CIVIL WAR
BATTLEGROUNDS

The Illustrated History
of the War's Pivotal
Battles and Campaigns

BATTLE SCENES, No. 1.

BATTLE *of* **WILSON'S CREEK,** MISSOURI.

BATTLE OF WILSON'S CREEK, MO., AUGUST 10, 1861. GEN. LYON LEADING INTO ACTION THE IOWA REGIMENT, WHOSE COLONEL HAD BEEN DISABLED.

BURNSIDE'S BRIGADE BULL RUN.

COL. BURNSIDE'S BRIGADE, FIRST AND SECOND RHODE ISLAND, AND SEVENTY-FIRST NEW YORK REGIMENTS, WITH THEIR ARTILLERY, ATTACKING THE REBEL BATTERIES AT BULL RUN.

THE THREE COMPANIES (F. C. & H.) OF THE FIRST Massachusetts, BULL RUN.

ATTACK ON THE BATTERIES AT BULL RUN BY THREE COMPANIES OF THE FIRST MASSACHUSETTS REGIMENT, LIEUTENANT-COLONEL WELLES, COMMANDING.

Published at H. H. LLOYD & CO.'S Agents' General Depot for Books, Maps, and Stationery Packages, 21 Howard Street, New York.

CIVIL WAR
BATTLEGROUNDS

The Illustrated History
of the War's Pivotal
Battles and Campaigns

Copyright © 2005 by Tehabi Books, Inc. and copyright © 2013 by Beckon Books, an imprint of Southwestern Publishing Group, 2451 Atrium Way, Nashville, TN 37214 USA.

This edition published in 2020 by Crestline,
an imprint of The Quarto Group
142 West 36th Street, 4th Floor
New York, NY 10018 USA
T (212) 779-4972 F (212) 779-6058
www.QuartoKnows.com

Portions of *Civil War Battlegrounds* was first published in 2005 by The Reader's Digest Association as *America's Battlegrounds*.

2013 edition, in commemoration of the 150th anniversary of the Civil War, published by Zenith Press,
an imprint of MBI Publishing Company, 400 1st Avenue North, Suite 400, Minneapolis, MN 55401 USA.

Crestline titles are also available at discount for retail, wholesale, promotional, and bulk purchase. For details, contact the Special Sales Manager by email at specialsales@quarto.com or by mail at The Quarto Group, Attn: Special Sales Manager, 100 Cummings Center Suite 265D, Beverly, MA 01915, USA.

10 9 8 7 6 5 4 3 2 1

Art Director: Vicky Vaughn Shea
Editor: Betsy Holt
Text: Richard Sauers, Ph.D. and Betsy Holt
On the title pages: Hand-colored lithograph of battles scenes. *Library of Congress*
Mourning for an assassinated president: a portrait of Lincoln attached to a black ribbon. *Library of Congress*

ISBN: 978-0-7858-3838-8

Printed in Singapore

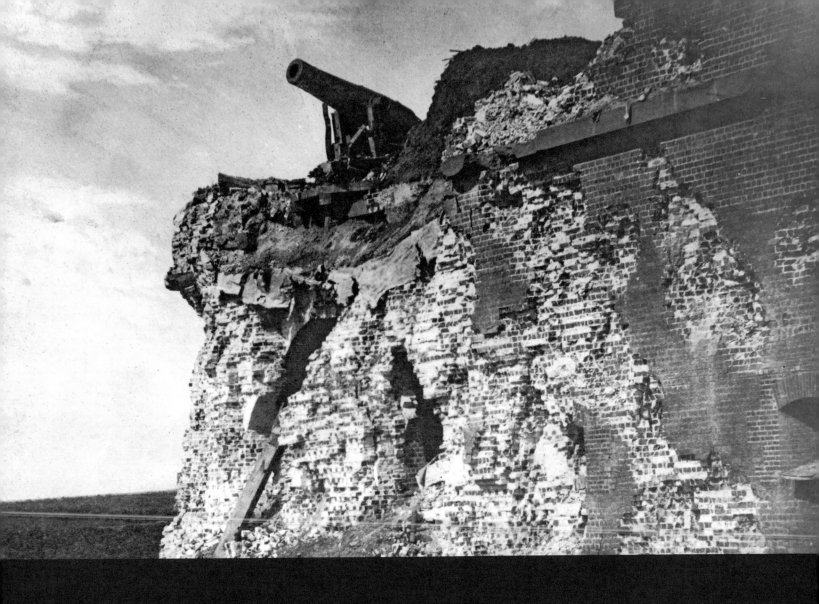

"The struggle of today is not altogether for today; it is for a vast future also. With a reliance on Providence, all the more firm and earnest, let us proceed in the great task which events have devolved upon us."

A lithograph of Pickett's Charge, which occurred on the third day of the Battle of Gettysburg, July 3, 1863

CONTENTS

This pro-Union print was produced as a complimentary presentation plate for the *Philadelphia Inquirer* in 1864. In it, Liberty wears a bronze breastplate and helmet, holding a sword in one hand and a Union flag and olive branch in the other. Justice leans to her right, and to her left sits Industry, depicted with a spindle and a small child in her lap.

LIBERTY.

"LIBERTY BRINGS TO THE EARTH JUSTICE AND PEACE"

PRESENTATION PLATE OF THE PHILADELPHIA INQUIRER.

1864.

INTRODUCTION

Benjamin Franklin once said that there was no such thing as a good war or a bad peace. But war has been almost a way of life for America. The United States was founded as a result of an armed revolution against Great Britain. A civil war in the 1860s held the nation together at a cost of over a million casualties. American involvement in two world wars spelled the difference between victory and defeat for the Western allies. Since World War II, American service-men and women have served abroad as guardians of world peace and order in a world increasingly divided by religion, politics, and ethnicity.

This book presents to the reader the most well-known and pivotal battlegrounds of the bloodiest war in our nation's history—the Civil War. Fought from 1861 to 1865, over

600,000 Union and Confederate soldiers lost their lives in nearly 400 battles on American soil. Many of the best known sites are administered by the United States government's National Park Service, while other sites are maintained by state and local agencies, as well as private initiatives.

We hope that this collection of words, maps, and illustrations will propel you to learn more about the important role that the Civil War played in American history and how this nation has commemorated the sacrifices of these Americans. All these sites are well worth a personal visit. They provide a stark reminder that freedom is not free.

This 1861 painting by William Bauly, *Fate of the Rebel Flag*, is the second in a pair of Unionist-themed works. In this scene, a burning warship, representing the Confederacy, sinks into the sea. The flames take on the configuration of an early Confederate flag, with seven stars representing the seceding states.

Captain William J. Hardee of the U.S. Army designed this black felt hat as the army's regulation dress hat. The blue hat cord and brass bugle together signify the infantry branch of service. During the Civil War, Hardee became a general in the Confederate Army.

THE CIVIL WAR

1861—1865

The seeds of civil war were sown by the U.S. Constitution, which recognized the existence of slavery and declared that five African Americans were equal to three white Americans for the purposes of representation in Congress. Throughout the first half of the nineteenth century, Northern states abolished slavery after abolitionist groups actively campaigned against the institution, using tactics such as the Underground Railroad to hide escaped slaves and openly defend escapees from pursuers who claimed their rights under the various fugitive slave laws enacted by Congress.

Civil War Union identification tag

THE LAST VETERAN

Walter Williams died on December 19, 1959. He claimed that he had served during the Civil War in a Texas regiment, and the nation mourned when he was laid to rest as the last survivor of the war. But research in pension records has shown that Walter Williams was not born until 1855 and could not possibly have served in the war. During the Great Depression, many aged men lacking money invented bogus stories of military service that were not investigated fully.

Recent research has shown that the last Confederate survivor was Pleasant Crump of the 10th Alabama, who died on December 31, 1951. The last bona fide survivor of the war was Albert Woolson, a drummer boy in the 1st Minnesota Heavy Artillery, who died on August 2, 1956. The Grand Army of the Republic erected a statue of Woolson at Gettysburg; a replica stands in Duluth, Minnesota, the soldier's postwar home.

Albert Woolson, the last legitimate veteran

By the 1850s, the North and South had begun to drift apart. The North was undergoing rapid industrialization, owing to new scientific advancements, while the South remained primarily agricultural, producing tobacco, cotton, pork, and other crops. Attacks from Northerners on the slave system met vigorous defenses by its advocates. This in turn resulted in exaggerated and often inaccurate views being held by the opposing sides about the other. Harriet Beecher Stowe's book *Uncle Tom's Cabin* further inflamed passions about the slave system.

Passions that were ignited by slavery extended to politics. Southern congressmen passionately defended their own interests and at times came to blows with Northerners in the Capitol building. South Carolina representative

Harriet Beecher Stowe, author of Uncle Tom's Cabin

John Brown

Preston Brooks's physical attack on Massachusetts senator Charles Sumner typified the rancor. The birth of the Republican Party in 1856 further exacerbated sectional rivalries. Having replaced the declining Whig Party, Republicans vigorously attacked slavery and advocated its eventual abolition.

Republicans wanted to limit slavery by preventing its expansion into western territories. This stance led to a de facto civil war in the Kansas Territory in 1854 as partisans of both sides flocked to the area, stuffed ballot boxes, armed themselves, and attacked their enemies. In 1859 abolitionist John Brown led an attack on the Federal arsenal at Harper's Ferry, Virginia. Brown wanted to use weapons stored there to arm slaves and incite a widespread rebellion. But his raid failed and

> ## "Though we fought beneath a scorching sun as well as scorching fire from the Confederates, the great Seven Days' fight is over, pictured in my mind as a terrible thunderstorm, with a goodly sprinkling of hail."
>
> —*Bates Alexander, 7th Pennsylvania Reserves*

Brown was hanged later that year.

These events presaged a presidential campaign in 1860 that was a watershed for the future of the nation. The Republicans chose Abraham Lincoln, an Illinois lawyer, as their candidate. Democrats could not agree and the party split into sectional wings; Northerners chose Stephen A. Douglas of Illinois and Southerners opted for John C. Breckinridge of Kentucky. Those disgusted with both sides formed the Constitutional Union Party, which

THE CIVIL WAR?

The name for the war in America that took place from 1861 to 1865 has been the subject of controversy ever since the guns stopped firing. Officially, the United States government called it the War of the Rebellion. But Southerners were apt to name it the War Between the States. Later, a compromise was reached when it was termed the Civil War. But partisans of both sides still have their own names for it—the War of Northern Aggression, the War of Southern Independence, the War for the Union, and the War of Secession, among them.

The Harper's Ferry Insurrection, 1859

CIVIL WAR CASUALTIES

Outdated battle tactics, modern weaponry, and widespread diseases combined to make the Civil War the bloodiest war in our nation's history. Deaths included 365,026 men in blue and perhaps 258,000 Confederates, a total of more than 623,000 soldiers. This total alone equals deaths in all American wars from the Revolution to Korea. A summary of American casualties:

Revolution	4,435*
War of 1812	2,260*
Mexican War	13,283
Civil War	623,026
Spanish-American War	2,446
World War I	116,708
World War II	407,316
Korean War	54,246
Vietnam War	57,685
Gulf War	269

*Total deaths are unknown; these figures represent only those killed in battle.

ran John Bell of Tennessee as its candidate. When the results were tallied, Lincoln, with only 40 percent of the popular vote, had received enough electoral votes to win the election. The other three candidates split the popular vote and made a Republican victory possible.

As a result of Lincoln's victory, South Carolinians declared that their state would leave the Union and form its own government to keep slavery safe. By the time Lincoln was sworn in as the nation's sixteenth president on March 4, 1861, several more states had joined South Carolina in forming the Confederacy, with former army officer and secretary of war Jefferson Davis as president. The new nation's Constitution was essentially a copy of the original document, and safeguarded slavery.

The Confederacy asked the new administration to remove its troops

Interior view of Fort Sumter

from Federal property in the South, most notably from Fort Sumter, which dominated Charleston Harbor. Lincoln, however, decided to keep the fort and ordered a relief expedition to bring more troops and supplies. To forestall this, Confederate batteries opened fire on the fort on April 12, 1861, triggering civil war. When Lincoln asked for 75,000 state militia to suppress the rebellion, the states of the upper South joined the Confederacy.

The resulting four years of sectional strife were pivotal in American history. More men were killed during these four years on American soil than at any other time in history. Troops still marched into battle arrayed in straight lines as in Napoleon's wars, but the advent of new weaponry meant that the old frontal assaults were suicidal, often resulting in horrendous casualties. The war saw the first sinking of a warship by a submarine, increasing use of entrenchments by defending troops, the use of railroads to move men and supplies, balloons for aerial reconnaissance, widespread use of the telegraph system to communicate more effectively, plus other new military innovations such as the Gatling gun.

Outnumbered, the South looked for diplomatic recognition from France and England, hoping that a shortage of cotton in Europe would tip the scales in its favor. Lincoln refused to recognize the Confederacy as a separate nation, thereby forestalling quick European intervention. Lincoln fought the war to preserve the Union, but in September 1862 he announced that if the Confederacy failed to surrender by January 1, 1863, all slaves in rebellious territory would be considered free. Thus, the war became a conflict to destroy slavery, ending any Confederate hope for foreign intervention.

The war's battles were generally fought in the South as Yankee armies invaded the Confederacy. In spite of being outnumbered, outstanding Southern generals like Robert E. Lee deflected Northern armies until 1864, when the simultaneous advance strategy advocated by Ulysses S. Grant, the new Union commanding general, wore down the South and prevented its armies from reinforcing one another. The capture of Atlanta in September 1864 by General

CIVIL WAR FIRSTS

The Civil War ushered in a new era of warfare. The CSS *Hunley* became the first submarine to sink an enemy vessel. Union artillery compelled the surrender of the brick-built Fort Pulaski in April 1862. Opposing ironclads dueled when CSS *Virginia* engaged USS *Monitor* in March 1862. Railroads and telegraphs improved communications, while the first wartime draft in the North spawned riots in New York City.

In 1862, the federal government enacted the first income tax. The government also began printing standard paper money and in 1863 passed a National Banking Act. With Southern Democrats out of Congress, progressive legislation that had been sidelined by the slavery issue came to the fore.

The 1862 Homestead Act regulated postwar westward expansion, while the Morrill Land Grant College Act provided money for states to establish public universities—Penn State and Texas A&M are just two that benefited from the transfer of western land. A transcontinental railroad bill legislated in 1862 came to fruition in 1869 with the driving of the "golden spike" at Promontory Point, Utah.

Confederate submarine CSS **Hunley**

The Chicago firm of Kurz & Allison introduced many thousands of Americans to the Civil War in the 1880s, when it issued a series of stylized prints of the war's great battles. This one, right, shows the death of Major General James B. McPherson at the battle of Atlanta on July 22, 1864. In reality, McPherson and an orderly rode into an advancing Confederate battle line and the general was shot from his horse when he ignored surrender demands and tried to gallop away.

Sherman helped ensure Lincoln's reelection and hastened the end of the war. When Confederate armies surrendered in the spring of 1865, Lincoln and Grant were in agreement not to punish the Rebels, but rather to let them go home to start life anew, thus avoiding guerilla warfare that might threaten the peace.

But Lincoln was assassinated by Southern sympathizer John Wilkes Booth at Ford's Theater only five days after Lee's surrender at Appomattox. Radical Republicans then dominated the new president, Andrew Johnson, and embarked on a campaign of hatred against the former Rebels. The era of Reconstruction had begun, but not as Lincoln would have wanted it to happen.

*This flag decorates the front
of the presidential box at
Ford's Theater.*

"With malice toward none, with charity for all, with firmness in the right as God gives us to see the right, let us strive on to finish the work we are in, to bind up the nation's wounds."

—Abraham Lincoln,
Second Inaugural Address,
March 4, 1865

Painted by Christopher Kimmel in 1861, *The Outbreak of Rebellion in the United States* is harshly critical of the Buchanan administration, Jefferson Davis, and the Confederacy. It shows Liberty at the center, flanked by Justice and Abraham Lincoln. James Buchanan, Lincoln's predecessor, sleeps at the foot of Liberty and Justice, while Confederate president Jefferson Davis stands beneath a palm tree flanked by a poisonous snake.

Name Fort Sumter

Classification National Monument

Established April 28, 1948

Contact 1214 Middle Street, Sullivan's Island, SC 29482

Phone 843-883-3123

Website www.nps.gov/fosu

Acreage 234.74 (all Federal)

Points of Focus Sally Port, Battery Huger, casements and cannons, Confederate Defender's Plaque, Liberty Square, Union Garrison Monument, Left-Flank Casemates, Enlisted Men's Barracks Ruins, Officers' Quarters Ruins, Parade Ground, Right-Gorge Angle, Mountain Howitzer, Esplanade, Granite Wharf Site

Tours/Paths Boat trip to Fort Sumter

Hours Visitor center open from 8:30 a.m. to 5:30 p.m. daily between April 1 and Labor Day. Closed Thanksgiving Day, December 25, and January 1

Park Fee $17 for adults; $15 for seniors; $10 for children ages 6 to 11

Programs Living History programs, interpretive talks, Junior Ranger program

Facilities Fort Sumter Visitor Education Center, museum, museum shop, and bookstore

Thomas Sumter

FORT SUMTER
WHERE THE CIVIL WAR BEGAN

Named for Revolutionary War hero Thomas Sumter, this five-sided brick fort controlled the entrance to Charleston Harbor. Workers had started construction in 1829 by building a man-made island in the middle of the harbor entrance, but in 1860, the fort was still unfinished. Most of the bastion's armaments had never been installed and only a small work force was generally on hand in the fort.

Charleston's main base was Fort Moultrie, where Kentucky-born Major Robert Anderson commanded the tiny garrison of the harbor. South Carolina seceded from the Union in December of 1860 and immediately began agitating for removal of Federal troops from its territory. Worried over its vulnerability to a surprise attack from local militia, Anderson abandoned Fort Moultrie on the night of December 26. His men rowed over to Fort Sumter and took possession, to the chagrin and anger of the city when it saw the American flag run up the fort's flagpole the next morning. Still, war had not yet erupted, and although the situation remained tense, Anderson continued to purchase supplies

Palmetto flag raised over Fort Sumter after its capture by Confederates on April 13, 1861

This dramatic Currier & Ives lithograph of the bombardment on April 12 and 13, 1861, exaggerates the rate of fire coming from Fort Sumter, whose guns limited their return fire to conserve ammunition.

"Our Southern brethren . . . have rebelled and have attacked their father's house. . . . They must be punished and brought back, but this necessity breaks my heart."

—Union Major Robert Anderson, after surrendering Fort Sumter, April 14, 1861

Sergeant Peter Hart returns the Fort Sumter flag to its staff after a Rebel cannonball smashed the wooden pole.

Interior of Fort Sumter during the Confederate bombardment

EDMUND RUFFIN

Born into the Virginia planter aristocracy, Edmund Ruffin (1794–1865) proved a failure in higher education and in a brief stint in the military in 1812. But he was very interested in the problems of soil infertility on his plantation and spent years working on an ultimately successful method to revitalize depleted soils. After writing an account of his work, Ruffin became publisher of the *Farmers Register* and established himself as a leading student of agriculture and soil science.

As war clouds gathered, Ruffin, who once asserted that slavery was an evil that had to be eliminated, changed his opinion and denounced Northern abolitionists. After South Carolina seceded from the Union, Ruffin moved to Charleston. Although he is often credited with the honor of firing the first shot against Fort Sumter on April 12, 1861, Ruffin's action was likely preceded by other cannon fire. Still, for his appearance in the fight, Ruffin was lionized throughout the South. He returned to Virginia once his home state had joined the Confederacy. After Lee surrendered, Ruffin's mental faculty quickly faded. On June 17, 1865, the aged Southerner committed suicide.

Private Edmund Ruffin

from local merchants even as his tiny force of 85 officers and men struggled to mount cannons found lying in the fort. Only 75 of the 135 prescribed for the fort were on hand.

When Abraham Lincoln was sworn in as president on March 4, 1861, he was approached by Southern commissioners seeking removal of Anderson's garrison. As the negotiations dragged on, Anderson began to run short of supplies after his local market was cut off. Lincoln therefore authorized a relief expedition to bring more troops and supplies to the fort. To avoid bloodshed, the president told South Carolinians of his intentions.

In answer, Confederate authorities demanded that Anderson surrender. When he refused, Confederate batteries opened fire at 4:30 in the morning on April 12, 1861. Fort Sumter's gunners began to reply after daybreak, but a

THE OTHER FORT

Fort Sumter was not the only fort retained by the U.S. government when Southern states began to secede. Between 1829 and 1834, the government erected Fort Pickens to protect the harbor of Pensacola, Florida. After Florida seceded in January 1861, Lieutenant Adam J. Slemmer evacuated other posts in the harbor and concentrated his men in Fort Pickens. He refused repeated surrender demands. Southern senators protested to President James Buchanan, who ordered Slemmer to maintain the garrison. An uneasy truce went into effect as both sides tried hard to avoid bloodshed. Union reinforcements arrived but remained aboard ships anchored near the fort in an effort to avoid angering the Confederates.

After Lincoln became president, he sent a navy lieutenant overland through the South with secret orders to land the troops. On April 12, the same day that war began in Charleston Harbor, Union troops strengthened Fort Pickens, ensuring that this vital fort would remain in Union hands. The fort today is part of the Gulf Islands National Seashore Park.

Confederate battery with gun pointed at Fort Sumter

Fort Pickens, Pensacola Harbor, Florida

shortage of men and ammunition limited Anderson's ability to engage in anything like a fair exchange of shells. Even though the Confederates expended more than 3,400 rounds, the bombardment caused little actual damage to the brick fort. The fort's barracks caught fire and burned during the bombardment, and a number of cannons were knocked out, but the garrison had only four men wounded. After 34 hours of fighting, and even as the Union relief expedition arrived off the harbor mouth but kept out of range of enemy shells, Anderson surrendered. The garrison was accorded the honors of war and was evacuated by the waiting Union ships. During the course of ceremonial gun firing, a cannon exploded accidentally and killed private Daniel Hough, who became the first fatality of the four-year Civil War.

Fort Sumter remained in Confederate hands for the rest of the war. In the summer of 1863, Union troops began siege operations against Charleston. By early September, the Yankees had gained control of Morris Island and had planted numerous batteries that fired on Fort Sumter. One massive 15-day bombardment blasted the fort, reducing it to rubble and leaving only a single cannon in working order. According to General P. G. T. Beauregard, "the crumbling of the masonry under the enemy's fire, converted this portion of Fort Sumter into a mass of debris and rubbish on which the enemy's powerful artillery could make but little impression."

Still, Fort Sumter's garrison, aided by other shore batteries, continued to repel Union naval attacks and even an attempted amphibious assault on the fort. By December 1863, Union gunners had thrown more than 26,000 rounds of ammunition into Sumter, but the fort continued to fly the Confederate flag. The garrison was evacuated as part of a general withdrawal in February 1865, when Union soldiers from the 52nd Pennsylvania planted their regimental colors on the debris. On April 14, 1865, four years to the day after he had surrendered the fort, Anderson returned to raise the same flag he had lowered in 1861.

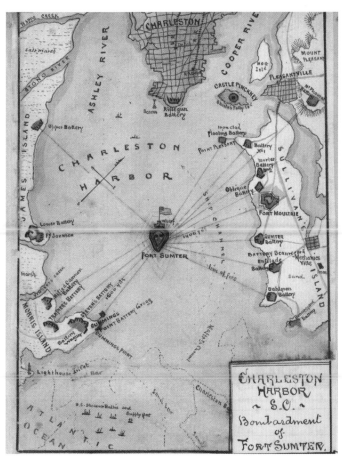

Fort Sumter and surrounding batteries

Civil War envelopes are sometimes thought of as precursors to modern-day postcards. Publication of these envelopes began in the mid-1850s, when the division between North and South became more pronounced, but halted before the end of the Civil War. Most of the envelopes were approximately three inches by five inches and featured illustrations of flags, Union and Confederate propaganda, and various political themes of the time period. The envelopes were published in nearly all of the major cities, with New York and Boston being the largest producers.

This Kurz & Allison print of First Manassas shows the rout of McDowell's Union Army. In the foreground, the dreaded Black Horse Cavalry attacks Union Zouaves as other troops cross Bull Run Bridge.

MANASSAS
TWO BATTLES AT BULL RUN

VISITOR INFORMATION

Name Manassas

Classification National Battlefield Park

Established May 10, 1940

Contact 12521 Lee Highway, Manassas, VA 20109

Phone 703-361-1339

Website www.nps.gov/mana

Acreage 5,073 (all Federal)

Points of Focus 1865 Monument, Jackson Monument on Henry House Hill, New York Zouaves Monuments, Stone Bridge, the Stone House, Brawner Farm Interpretive Center

Tours/Paths Three self-guided walking tours, 13-mile driving tour of Second Battle of Manassas, Electronic Battle map, Ranger-guided walking tour (summer season only)

Hours Visitor center open daily from 8:30 a.m. to 5:00 p.m. Closed Thanksgiving Day and December 25. The Brawner Farm Interpretive Center is open daily from 10:00 a.m. to 4:30 p.m. through the end of November. Closed on Thanksgiving Day.

Park Fee $3 for 3-day pass; $20 for annual pass; $80 Interagency Annual Pass; free for visitors ages 16 and under

Programs 45-minute battle film ($3 fee)

Facilities Visitor center, Stuart's Hill Center, museum, bookstore, picnic area

In the early days of the war when President Lincoln issued a call for 75,000 militia to suppress the Southern rebellion, the troops enlisted for a period of three months. That was presumed long enough to crush the new Confederacy, but the slow pace of training and gathering troops showed the administration that three months was insufficient. In order not to waste the thousands of troops already enlisted, in April 1861, Brigadier General Irvin McDowell, commander of Federal troops around Washington, was pressured into mounting an offensive to disperse the

Ruins of Mrs. Judith Henry's house. Henry was the only civilian killed during the battle.

enemy in front of him. McDowell would next march south to capture Richmond, capital of the Confederacy.

McDowell had about 35,000 men available after detaching guards for the forts being constructed around Washington. The general planned to engage 22,000 Rebels under the command of Brigadier General P. G. T. Beauregard before the enemy received reinforcements. A second Union force led by Pennsylvania militia general Robert Patterson would cross the Potomac at Harper's Ferry and advance up the Shenandoah Valley toward Winchester, which was then being defended

MANASSAS NATIONAL BATTLEFIELD PARK ★ MANASSAS, VIRGINIA

WILMER McLEAN

Wilmer McLean was an average farmer living in northern Virginia when the Civil War erupted in 1861. His farmhouse was used by Confederate general P. G. T. Beauregard as headquarters when the Confederate army assembled near Bull Run to confront the Union advance from Washington. During the battle of First Manassas, a Union artillery projectile hit the kitchen, reputedly as dinner was being cooked. His farm disrupted by the war, McLean moved his family far to the southwest to the little village of Appomattox Court House, where he bought a house and continued his work as a sugar speculator until April 1865.

When General Lee decided to discuss surrender terms with Grant, McLean offered the use of his spacious two-story brick house. It was in McLean's parlor that Grant and Lee signed the surrender terms that ended the war in Virginia. But then McLean saw his parlor ruined by souvenir seekers. General Custer bought a wooden stand and presented it as a gift to General Sheridan's wife. Other officers simply walked off with souvenirs. Even the trees outside the house were whittled away by Union soldiers anxious for something to take home. McLean later sold the house and returned to the Manassas area.

After Grant's reelection as president in 1872 McLean worked as a government employee until his death in 1882. The current McLean House in the park at Appomattox is a reconstruction of the original.

by 12,000 Confederates under the command of General Joseph E. Johnston.

THE FIRST BATTLE OF MANASSAS

McDowell's troops left Washington on July 16 and moved forward to Bull Run, a small stream that crossed the front of Beauregard's troops. After reconnoitering the area, McDowell decided to send a

General Irvin McDowell

column upstream to outflank the Rebels rather than attacking across the creek. However, unknown to McDowell, General Johnston had already arrived and was followed by the first contingents of his troops from Winchester. Patterson had moved slowly and Johnston began sending his troops by train to Manassas Junction, a short march from Bull Run.

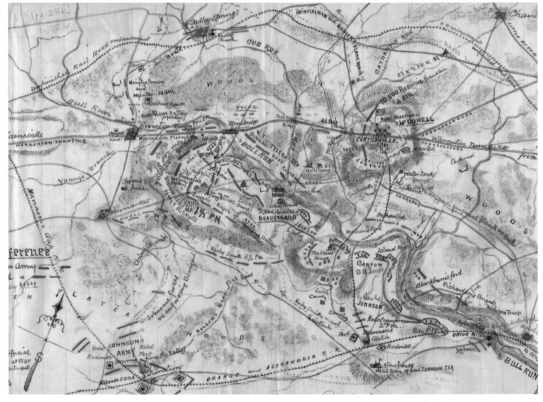

Movement of the Union and Confederate forces on July 21, 1861, during the First Battle of Manassas, or Bull Run

Confederate fortifications, Manassas, Virginia, March 1862

McDowell's flanking column set out before dawn on July 21. The brigades crossed Bull Run and struck the Confederate left flank, driving the defenders slowly back. But Confederate signalmen had detected the Union maneuver and Beauregard began shifting the majority of his army to face the oncoming Yankees. By noon, Union troops attacking along the front had put enough pressure on the Southerners to cause their lines to waver and retreat. As Rebels fell back across the broad plateau of Henry House Hill, General Thomas J. Jackson's brigade of Virginians waited in reserve to face the Yankees. Noticing Jackson sitting calmly on his horse, General Bernard E. Bee called to his retreating troops, "Look! There stands Jackson like a stone wall! Rally behind the Virginians!"

Thus was born one of the war's most famous nicknames.

Federal regiments repeatedly attacked Jackson's position only to be thrown back by the defenders. More Southern troops arrived on the battlefield, some having just arrived by train from Winchester. Both sides were tired from fighting in the hot July sun that afternoon. When the 53rd Virginia, clothed in blue uniforms, fired a destructive volley into massed Federal artillery, the Union attacks finally began to falter. Southern reinforcements began to advance, and McDowell ordered a retreat. When a Southern shell crashed into a wagon that overturned on the Cub Run bridge, the retreat began to degenerate into a rout as tired and dispirited Yankees threw away their equipment, broke ranks, and

"In a few moments our entire line was engaged in a fierce and sanguinary struggle with the enemy. As one line was repulsed, another took its place and pressed forward as if determined by force of numbers and fury of assault to drive us from our positions."

—*Confederate Major General Stonewall Jackson*

JOHN POPE

In 1861, Captain John Pope was one of four officers assigned to escort Lincoln to Washington, DC, for his inauguration. He was promoted to brigadier general and served in the Mississippi Valley, capturing Island Number 10 in March 1862. Pope was then promoted to major general and brought east to command the new Army of Virginia. A braggart by nature, Pope announced that his headquarters would be in the saddle; Southern wags quickly said that his headquarters were where his hindquarters ought to be.

After the defeat at Second Manassas, Pope was assigned to the Department of the Northwest, where he crushed the Sioux uprising. Following the Civil War, he served on the frontier against Native Americans. The general went against the grain at the time by seeking administration of reservations by the military instead of by the corrupt Indian Bureau. Pope came to admire Native Americans and called for their more humane and honorable treatment.

General John Pope

". . . at the spot where my company fought I counted where 20 balls had struck a white oak not much larger than a man's body, and nearly all within six feet of the ground. Not a bush had been missed. . . . It seems marvelous how many of us escaped being killed."

—*Captain Walter W. Lenoir, 37th North Carolina*

ran. Rumors of Confederate cavalry in pursuit hastened the disorganized retreat to Washington. During the panic, civilians from Washington who had come to the front to see the battle were scooped up as prisoners, including one congressman. But the Confederates were too disorganized to pursue. Casualties totaled some 2,896 for McDowell and 1,982 for the Confederates, who had won the first important battle of the war.

THE SECOND BATTLE OF MANASSAS

A year later, Manassas was the scene of another encounter between blue and gray. After Major General George B. McClellan's failure to capture Richmond, the War Department united the scattered Union forces in and around Washington and the Shenandoah Valley as the Army of Virginia. Major General John Pope,

fresh from victories in the Mississippi Valley, was placed in command. General Robert E. Lee detached Stonewall Jackson's corps to counter any move Pope might make. On August 9, Jackson engaged one of Pope's corps in battle at Cedar Mountain, south of Culpeper.

Once Lee received news that McClellan's troops were being evacuated from the Peninsula and sent north to reinforce Pope, he decided that Pope must be attacked and defeated before the two Union armies united their strength. So General James Longstreet's corps was also sent to join Jackson. While Longstreet advanced, Jackson proposed to Lee that he would circle around behind Pope's army, interdict his supplies, and force Pope to either fight at a disadvantage or retreat to Washington. The result was the campaign of Second Manassas.

Jackson's corps began to march around Pope's right flank on August 25. Two days later, the Confederates swooped down on Pope's supply base at Manassas Junction, burning whatever they could not carry away. Pope misused his mounted troops and sent his infantry searching for the elusive Confederates, who took position in an unfinished railroad bed adjoining the old Manassas battlefield. Once Jackson received word that Longstreet was marching to join him, he attacked some of Pope's troops at Brawner's Farm early in the evening of August 28.

Alerted to Jackson's whereabouts, Pope began to collect his army and during the day on August 29 hurled his troops in a series of uncoordinated assaults on Jackson's strong position. Although outnumbered and faced with defeat if the Federals were to break through, Jackson's men grimly hung on. Late in the day, Longstreet's troops began to form on Jackson's right flank. Union probing attacks revealed the presence of more Confederates, but Pope refused to believe the reports. He firmly maintained that Jackson had been beaten and was preparing to withdraw. Pope's orders for August 30 called for a pursuit of Jackson's men; even though his generals tried to advise him of the true state of affairs, Pope disbelieved them. As a result, his attacks were again repelled and later in the afternoon, Lee unleashed Longstreet's corps in a decisive attack against Pope's left flank.

Longstreet's charge drove in Pope's left and forced the Yankees to call in reinforcements to blunt the force of the attack even as Pope's troops began a retreat to Washington. The two-day battle of Second Manassas was followed by a sharp encounter at Chantilly on September 1 as Jackson tried to cut into the retreating Union columns, but was repulsed. The battles cost Pope 16,054 casualties as opposed to a loss of 9,197 Southern troops, and Pope's retreat paved the way for Lee's invasion of Maryland.

Dedication of the Manassas Battle Monument

MANASSAS

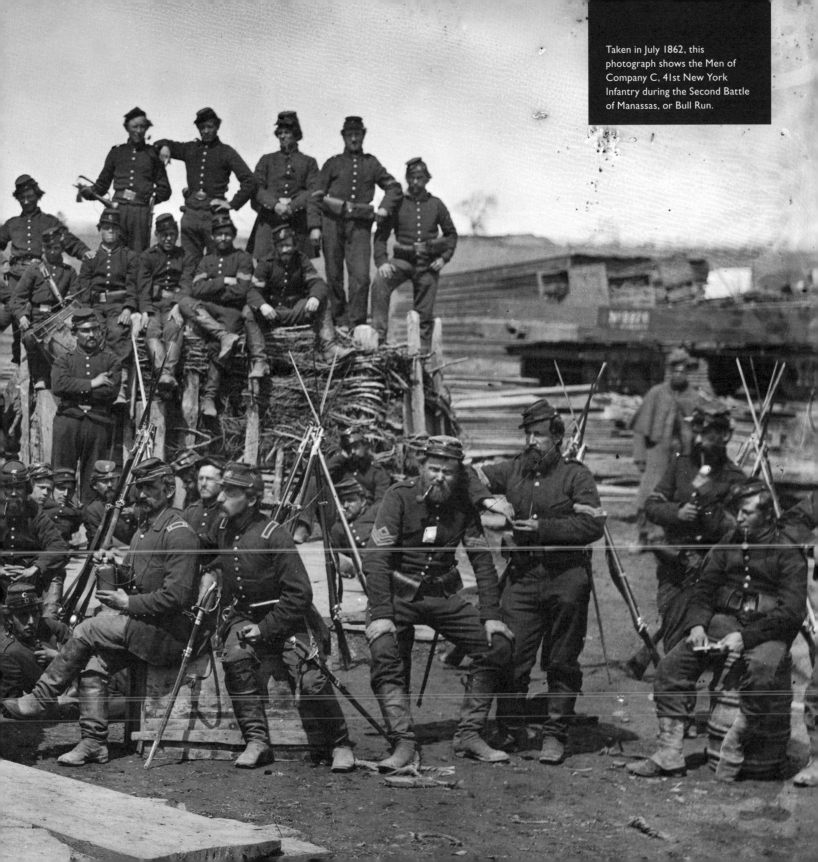

Taken in July 1862, this photograph shows the Men of Company C, 41st New York Infantry during the Second Battle of Manassas, or Bull Run.

WILSON'S CREEK

BLOODY BATTLE IN MISSOURI

Missouri was divided as the Civil War began. Although Governor Claiborne Jackson was pro-Southern, a substantial German population in St. Louis and elsewhere remained staunchly loyal to the Union. Union Brigadier General Nathaniel Lyon neutralized pro-Southern militia units, seized Jefferson City, then followed the fleeing governor into southwest Missouri, where General Sterling Price was assembling an army of Missourians to regain the state for the Confederacy.

By mid-July 1861, Lyon had advanced to Springfield, where he learned that he was badly outnumbered. Price had been reinforced by Arkansas and Louisiana troops; his army now numbered about 12,000 men. Undaunted, Lyon decided to attack. Leaving a thousand men to guard his supplies, Lyon detached Colonel Franz Sigel and his brigade of 1,200 men to circle behind Price's encampments along Wilson's Creek, 10 miles southwest of Springfield. Lyon planned to launch a frontal assault with 4,300 men, hoping to surprise and panic Price's raw recruits.

On the morning of August 10, Lyon's force emerged from the morning mist to rout the troops in Price's first encampments. Lyon's column forged ahead and occupied the crest of a low ridge before grinding to a halt when Confederate

Union Brigadier General Nathaniel Lyon is mortally wounded by Confederate rifle fire during the Battle of Wilson's Creek, Missouri. Samuel D. Sturgis, replacing Lyon, ordered a retreat to Springfield. The Confederates were unable to follow up this tactical victory, allowing the Union to maintain control of southwestern Missouri.

Did You Know?

The Battle of Wilson's Creek, which took place on August 10, 1861, was the first major Civil War battle fought west of the Mississippi River. There, ardent Unionist Nathaniel Lyon died at the age of forty-three—the first Union general killed in the war. Although the Union lost, it maintained control of Missouri, which became one of the most fought-after states in the nation. After the battle, Lyon's body was carried in an elaborate funeral procession to his home in Connecticut.

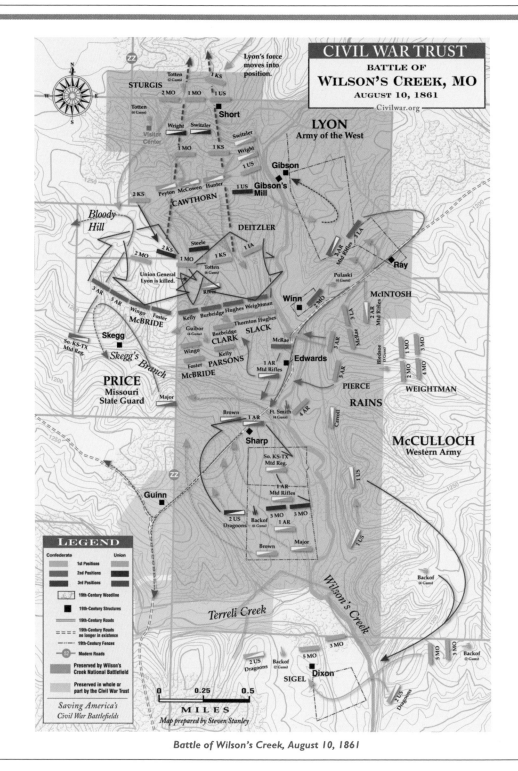

Battle of Wilson's Creek, August 10, 1861

General Lyon leads his men into battle.

artillery opened fire. Meanwhile, upon hearing the noise of Lyon's attack, Sigel opened fire on unsuspecting Confederates in camps in front of him. After some initial success, Sigel mistakenly allowed an enemy unit to approach close to his line and fire a volley. His men abandoned their artillery and fled.

Sigel's failure allowed the Confederates to concentrate their efforts on Lyon's troops. The fighting on the ridge, nicknamed Bloody Hill by the combatants, was obstinate and fierce. Lyon's men repelled three attacks before Lyon, already twice wounded, was killed. Major Samuel D. Sturgis then authorized a withdrawal, his men being outnumbered and short on ammunition. Price did not pursue. Casualties totaled 1,317 for the Federals and 1,222 for the Confederates. While Wilson's Creek was a tactical Confederate victory, Lyon's bold gamble delayed Confederate plans and in the long run helped secure Missouri for the Union.

> "It was in our front here . . . that the brave commander of the Federal forces, General Lyon, was killed, gallantly leading his men to what he and they supposed was victory, but which proved . . . disastrous defeat. In the light of the present day, even, it is difficult to measure the vast results had Lyon lived."
>
> —Union Brigadier General N. B. Pearce

A scene from the Battle of Fort Donelson shows Union soldiers assembling near an overly stylized fort. Indecision on the part of the Confederate generals allowed Grant to drive them back into the fort and force a mass surrender.

FORT DONELSON

UNCONDITIONAL SURRENDER

VISITOR INFORMATION

Name Fort Donelson

Classification National Battlefield

Established March 26, 1928

Contact P.O. Box 434, Dover, TN 37058

Phone 931-232-5706

Website www.nps.gov/fodo

Acreage 1,007 (Federal: 943; Nonfederal: 64)

Points of Focus Confederate Monument, Dover Hotel, Forge Road, French Battery, Jackson's Battery, Log Huts, National Cemetery, River Batteries

Tours/Paths 5.7 miles of hiking trails, self-guided walking tour

Hours Visitor center open daily from 8:00 a.m. to 4:30 p.m. Closed December 25. Surrender House open daily from 8:15 a.m. to 4:00 p.m.

Park Fee Free

Programs Audiovisual introductory program, Junior Ranger program, First Bloom program

Facilities Visitor center, museum, bookstore

In February 1862, the Union high command approved a joint army-navy attack on Forts Henry and Donelson, two Southern earthwork forts that controlled traffic on the Tennessee and Cumberland Rivers. General Ulysses S. Grant was in command of the army troops while Flag Officer Andrew H. Foote led a flotilla of four ironclads and two wooden gunboats. Fort Henry fell to the Union navy on February 6.

Grant's men were in position to attack Fort Donelson on February 13. His 15,000 soldiers were opposed by approximately 20,000 Southerners under the command of General John B. Floyd, a former U.S. Secretary of War from Virginia. Foote's armored ships attacked on February 13, but his slow-moving vessels were repeatedly hit by shells and forced to retreat. Foote himself was badly wounded and later died from his injuries.

In the meantime Grant had almost surrounded the Confederate earthworks with his troops. Floyd was determined to break out and retreat to avoid a siege. The Rebels attacked Grant's right flank early on the morning of February 15 and were initially

Fort Donelson water battery

Flag Officer Andrew H. Foote

FORT DONELSON NATIONAL BATTLEFIELD ★ DOVER, TENNESSEE

Did You Know?

The Confederate army's surrender of Fort Donelson on February 16, 1862, represented the first great Union victory. It also created a Union hero in Ulysses S. Grant. When Grant received a note from Confederate commanders, who were hoping to negotiate, he replied brusquely: "No terms except an unconditional and immediate surrender can be accepted." Grant was subsequently promoted to major general.

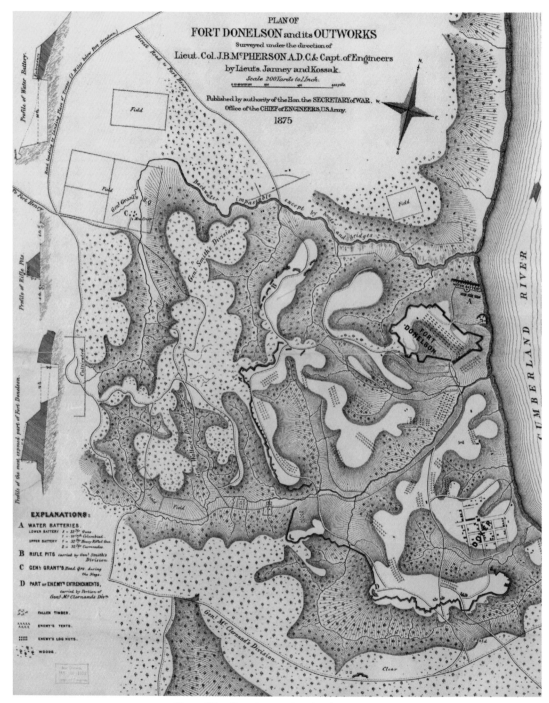

Plan of Fort Donelson and its fortifications

successful. But then indecision and delay on Floyd's part gave Grant the opportunity to bring up more troops, counterattack, and drive the enemy back into their fortifications.

That night Floyd decided to abandon his command; he placed his Virginia regiments on transport vessels and steamed away. He was afraid that if captured he might be tried for treason. His second in command, General Gideon J. Pillow, followed suit and turned command of the fort over to General Simon B. Buckner, a Kentuckian who had joined the Confederacy.

That evening more Yankee reinforcements arrived, giving Grant 27,000 soldiers. On the sixteenth, Buckner hoisted a white flag and asked for terms. "No terms except unconditional and immediate surrender can be accepted," replied Grant. Buckner accepted, and

15,000 Confederates were taken prisoner. The press quickly nicknamed the Union general "Unconditional Surrender Grant," whose twin victories had forced a Confederate withdrawal from most of Tennessee. Grant was promoted from brigadier general to major general, and a legend was born.

General Ulysses S. Grant's plan for the attack and capture of Fort Donelson

"Fort Donelson will hereafter be marked in Capitals on the maps of our United Country, and the men who fought the battle will live in the memory of a grateful people."

—Union General Ulysses S. Grant

VISITOR INFORMATION

Name Pea Ridge

Classification National Military Park

Established July 20, 1956

Contact 15930 E. Highway 62 Garfield, AR 72732

Phone 479-451-8122

Website www.nps.gov/peri

Acreage 4,300.35 (Federal: 4,278.75; Nonfederal: 21.60)

Points of Focus Elkhorn Tavern, Leetown Battlefield, Pratt's Store, Telegraph/Military Road, West Overlook

Tours/Paths 7-mile self-guided driving tour, hiking trails, horse trails, interpretive exhibits

Hours Visitor Center hours open daily from 8:30 a.m. to 4:30 p.m. Closed Thanksgiving, December 25, and January 1

Park Fee $5 per person; $5 per motorcycle; $10 per vehicle; $20 annual pass per person. Fees are valid for 7 days

Programs 28-minute orientation film, Junior Ranger program

Facilities Visitor center, museum, picnic area, recreational park (requires additional entry fee), bookstore

PEA RIDGE

MISSOURI SAVED FOR THE UNION

After the Union defeat at Wilson's Creek, Missouri, in August 1861, General Samuel R. Curtis took command and embarked on an offensive in February 1862. His troops maneuvered Sterling Price's men out of Missouri into northwestern Arkansas before the Confederate government sent Benjamin McCulloch's troops to reinforce Price. But these two commanders bickered with each other, and the aggressive General Earl Van Dorn was placed in command of the joint army,

General Samuel R. Curtis

which included 1,000 Native Americans.

Van Dorn decided to counter Curtis's offensive with his own. He outnumbered Curtis slightly: 14,000 to 11,000. Curtis took position behind Little Sugar Creek, his men building earthworks to defend the creek. Behind them lay the high ground known as Pea Ridge.

Rather than assail Curtis's strong position, Van Dorn embarked on a bold plan. He divided his army in half and sent Price's Missourians on a march behind Pea Ridge to Elkhorn Tavern, where his men might block Curtis's

PEA RIDGE NATIONAL MILITARY PARK ★ PEA RIDGE, ARKANSAS

Kurz & Allison capture essential elements of the Pea Ridge battle in this lithograph. Union artillery was instrumental in this fight, discouraging Price's Native American units and paving the way for Curtis's success on the second day of the battle.

"I am now in for it, to make a reputation and serve my country conspicuously or fail."

—Confederate Major
General Earl Van Dorn,
before the battle at Pea Ridge

retreat route. Meanwhile, McCulloch's troops would attack the Union right flank from the direction of Leetown, a small village south of Pea Ridge. Threatened to his right and rear, Curtis would have to withdraw or be annihilated.

Curtis was soon aware of Van Dorn's movements and reacted swiftly. On March 7, 1862, one of his divisions went to Elkhorn Tavern and fought Price's troops to a standstill while his other units engaged McCulloch's column. McCulloch was killed during the confused fighting and the roar of Yankee artillery discouraged his Native American allies. After dark, McCulloch's survivors moved to Elkhorn Tavern, where they joined Price's men. Van Dorn decided against retreat and hoped to confront Curtis again on March 8.

An 1862 Currier & Ives lithograph depicting the Battle of Pea Ridge

Curtis obliged Van Dorn by attacking after his artillery silenced their counterparts, and on March 9, Van Dorn ordered a retreat. Curtis suffered a loss of 1,384 and Van Dorn more than 2,000 in the two-day Battle of Pea Ridge, also known as Elkhorn Tavern. But Van Dorn's retreat meant that Missouri was safe from invasion for the foreseeable future.

Reconstructed Elkhorn Tavern

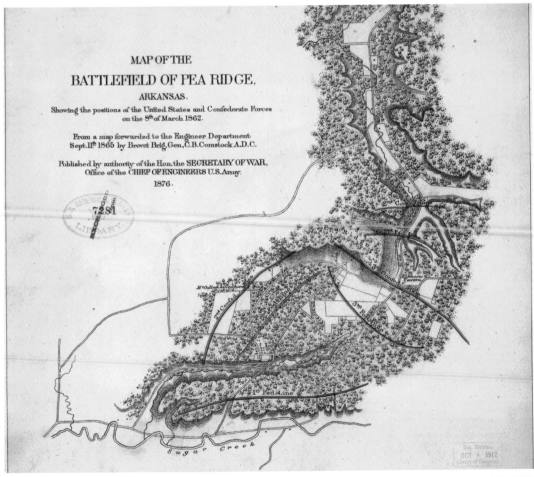
Map of the battlefield of Pea Ridge, showing the positions of the Union and Confederate soldiers on March 8, 1862

Did You Know?

During the battle of Pea Ridge—which saved the hotly contested state of Missouri for the Union—the Southerners attacked from the north, and the Northerners attacked from the south. It was the only major battle in which Native American troops participated and one of the few in which the Confederate troops outnumbered the Union soldiers. Today, Pea Ridge is the most intact battlefield in the United States.

Thousands of graves of Civil War soldiers are simply marked as "Unknown." The army issued no dog tags, and many soldiers carried no identification. When slain in battle, many men were buried near where they fell and often moved years later to proper cemeteries.

SHILOH

THE WAR'S FIRST BLOODBATH

After the capture of Forts Henry and Donelson in February 1862, Brigadier General Ulysses S. Grant's Federal troops, named the Army of the Tennessee, moved up the Tennessee River to a place called Pittsburgh Landing, barely 23 miles from Corinth, Mississippi, the main Confederate supply base. Grant's successful campaign had unhinged the Confederate defensive line for Kentucky and Tennessee. Rebel troops retreated south to Corinth even as Union general Don Carlos Buell's troops marched into Nashville. Major General Henry W. Halleck, in command of Union troops west of the Appalachian Mountains, ordered Grant to remain at Pittsburgh Landing until Buell moved to join him. Then the combined armies would seize Corinth.

Major General Henry W. Halleck

Confederate general Albert Sidney Johnston was in charge of the Rebel troops opposing Grant. He assembled 40,000 men at Corinth, organized them as the Army of the Mississippi, and moved north to attack Grant before Buell's troops reached the area. Johnston realized that if Buell arrived first, he would be badly outnumbered and unable to resist the combined Union armies.

AN ARMY COMMANDER'S STRANGE DEATH

Albert Sidney Johnston directed the Confederate attack on Grant's camps at Shiloh. Later that day, the general witnessed repeated Confederate attacks against the Union defenders of the "Hornet's Nest" area of the battlefield. Sometime during the fighting, Johnston was hit by a minié ball in the back of his right leg. Johnston had suffered a wound during a duel in 1837 and his right leg was generally numb to heat, cold, and pain. Tennessee governor Isham Harris, one of Johnston's aides, had just returned from a mission when the general reeled in the saddle. Harris helped Johnston to the ground and sent for his physician, who had left to help tend wounded men of both armies. Harris was unable to find a wound except for the gunshot wound in Johnston's leg, which was easily treatable if quickly located. But Johnston must have been shot minutes earlier and his knee-high boot had filled with blood, which he seemingly did not notice in the heat of combat. Johnston soon died from an acute loss of blood; the bullet had severed an artery and he bled to death. Ironically, a tourniquet was found in his coat pocket. If used properly, it would have saved his life.

General A. S. Johnston

"The battle now raged with indescribable fury . . . the roar of the artillery, and the incessant rattle of the small arms."

—*Peter W. Alexander, correspondent for the* Savannah Republican, *April 18, 1862*

Johnston's advance troops neared the Union lines on April 5. Union pickets quickly realized the enemy was in the woods in front of their camps and reported their discovery. However, Grant's subordinates discounted these reports, which they felt were the exaggerated imaginings of inexperienced soldiers.

Johnston ordered an advance early on the morning of Sunday, April 6. The initial Confederate assaults by William J. Hardee's corps struck the

General Benjamin M. Prentiss (mounted) directs the fighting at Hornet's Nest.

Yankee encampments of divisions led by William T. Sherman and Benjamin M. Prentiss. Some men in blue were literally caught with their pants down as Confederates achieved surprise in their initial attacks. The forward Union camps were captured as their occupants alternately fled, rallied, and retreated under enemy pressure.

By 10:30 a.m., Prentiss had managed to rally much of his division and took position along an old wagon road about a mile to the rear. Other units formed on his flanks as Yankees continued to retreat to a series of high bluffs overlooking Pittsburgh Landing. Grant, headquartered on a troop transport, had arrived and was endeavoring to form a defensive line as a last stand. But the Confederates were as much disorganized by victory as the Yanks were by defeat. The wooded terrain had disrupted lines of battle, and many starved Southerners had fallen out of line to pillage the

General Ulysses S. Grant rallying his troops during the Battle of Shiloh

abandoned Union camps.

However, shortly after noon, Braxton Bragg's Confederate troops began the first of a series of attacks on Prentiss's position. After two hours of piecemeal attacks, Prentiss still held his ground, but he was in danger of being cut off from Grant's still-forming line in his rear. The action centered on what soldiers called the "Hornet's Nest," where the fighting was protracted and bloody. General Johnston personally was in the fray here, encouraging his men and sending in reinforcements. But the general was shot in

Did You Know?

At the Battle of Shiloh—one of the bloodiest battles in American history—two future presidents fought for the Union army: Ulysses S. Grant, the eighteenth president, and James A. Garfield, the twentieth president. Other notable veterans of Shiloh included explorer John Wesley Powell, a Union artillery officer who lost his arm during the battle, and Confederate army commander, General Albert Sidney Johnston, who lost his life at Shiloh and is still the highest ranking American military officer to be killed in action.

Recapture of artillery by a portion of General Lovell H. Rosseau's command on April 7, 1862

> **"There arose the severest musketry I ever heard. . . ."**
>
> —*Union General William Tecumseh Sherman*

his right leg as he led men into battle. He dismissed the injury at first, but then bled to death because the bullet had severed a vital artery. General P. G. T. Beauregard then assumed command of the Confederate army.

By six o'clock, continued Rebel assaults finally overwhelmed Prentiss, who surrendered with the remnants of his division. But his holding action of five hours delayed active Confederate attacks elsewhere, enabling Grant to deploy artillery batteries and rally the other

divisions. Two Union wooden gunboats, *Lexington* and *Tyler*, also arrived and threw shells into the Confederate lines. At dusk, Beauregard sent in an attack on the new line, which repelled the Southerners. The enemy then withdrew to rest and prepare to continue the battle the next day.

That night, however, Lew Wallace's division arrived on the battlefield and four of Buell's divisions were ferried across the river to join Grant's survivors. At dawn on April 7, Grant and Buell sent their troops forward to recapture lost ground. The relentless Union attack rolled forward and drove back Beauregard's tired men. Sometime around 3:30, Beauregard ordered a retreat. Many of his regiments were out of ammunition and his troops were now badly outnumbered by the combined Union armies. The Yankees failed to pursue the Rebels. Cavalry led by Nathan Bedford Forest skillfully covered the retreat, which was hampered by a heavy overnight rain.

This Battle of Shiloh, so named for a small log meeting house on the battlefield, was shocking news to families across the divided country. Grant's losses totaled 13,047, while the Confederates counted 10,699 casualties. The blood-bath at Shiloh was only a precursor of battles to come, but its severity and long casualty lists appalled both sides. Critics of Lincoln's administration called for Lincoln to fire Grant.

Newspapers reported that the general had been drunk and mishandled the fighting. In response, Lincoln reputedly asked what brand of whiskey Grant used; he wished to send some to those of his generals who refused to fight.

In the end, Halleck personally came to the front and took command, relegating Grant to a subordinate role as second in command. The cautious Halleck brought in more troops and in early May began a slow movement toward Corinth. Worried about surprise attacks, the general ordered earthworks erected every night to protect his camps. By May 25, his men had

finally approached the Corinth defenses. Beauregard, outnumbered more than two to one, evacuated the city and retreated. Corinth was occupied by Halleck's troops on May 30 and remained in Union hands for the rest of the war.

Movement of the Union and Confederate forces on April 6, 1862, the first day of the Battle of Shiloh

LEWIS WALLACE

Lew Wallace (1827–1905) was an Indiana lawyer who wore many different hats during the war. He raised the 11th Indiana in 1861, served briefly as the state's adjutant general, and commanded one of Grant's divisions at Shiloh. His command was several miles away when the fighting started. Wallace received orders to march to the battlefield, but his orders seemed unclear; his troops got lost and were only on hand for the second day of the battle. Wallace lost his command as a result, but in 1864 was placed in command of the Union's Middle Department. His troops delayed Jubal Early's march on Washington at the Battle of Monocacy.

Lewis Wallace

This 1885 print depicts the bloody Battle of Shiloh on April 6, 1862. Losses numbered in the tens of thousands for both the Union and Confederate armies.

VISITOR INFORMATION

Name Fort Pulaski

Classification National Monument

Established October 15, 1924. Transferred from War Department August 10, 1933. Boundary changes: June 26, 1936; May 25, 1959

Contact P.O. Box 30757 Highway 80, East Savannah, GA 31410

Phone 912-786-5787

Website www.nps.gov/fopu

Acreage 5,623.10 (Federal: 5,365.13; Nonfederal: 257.97)

Points of Focus Battery Halleck, Cockspur Island, Construction Village, McQueens Island, Historic Dike System

Tours/Paths Self-guided walking tour, hiking trails, North Pier trail, Lighthouse overlook trail

Hours Visitor center open daily from 9:00 a.m. to 5:00 p.m. (in the summer from 9:00 a.m. to 6:30 p.m.). Closed Thanksgiving Day and December 25

Park Fee $5 per person ages 16 and up; free for visitors ages 15 and under. Group rates available

Programs 17-minute orientation film, interpretive programs, Junior Ranger program

Facilities Visitor center, picnic area, bookstore

FORT PULASKI
THE END OF BRICK FORTS

Named for Revolutionary War hero Count Casimir Pulaski, this five-sided brick fort guarded the water approaches to the Georgia port city of Savannah. Located on Cockspur Island at the mouth of the Savannah River, Fort Pulaski's defenses would repel any seaborne attack against Savannah. The fort, with its 7½-foot-thick brick walls, had been constructed between 1829 and 1847 at a cost of over a million dollars.

When Georgia seceded from the Union in 1861, militia seized the fort and quickly brought it up to battle readiness, mounting 48 of a possible 140 cannons that could be positioned inside the bastion. Colonel Charles H. Olmstead, in command of the 1st Georgia regiment, was placed in charge of defending the fort.

In November 1861, a Union army–navy expedition attacked and captured the Confederate forts guarding

Fort Pulaski after it was captured by Union troops in April 1862

FORT PULASKI NATIONAL MONUMENT ★ SAVANNAH, GEORGIA

The walls of Fort Pulaski that faced Union bombardment suffered heavy damage. This view shows the interior at one of the casements in the fort's lower tier of guns. Rubble from the blasted wall made this gun all but useless. Union soldiers later repaired most of the damage, and the fort remained a key Federal position.

Hilton Head, South Carolina, placing the Yankees within striking distance of Fort Pulaski. Union general Quincy A. Gillmore planned to capture the fort. His infantry occupied Tybee Island and installed 26 smoothbores and 10 newer rifled pieces such as 30-pounder Parrotts. Union batteries were located from 1,650 to 3,400 yards from the fort. When his batteries were ready, Gillmore sent a flag of truce to Colonel Olmstead, demanding a surrender to avoid bloodshed. "I am here to defend the fort, not to surrender it," was Olmstead's heroic reply.

Thus, Gillmore's cannons opened fire on the morning of April 10, 1862. Bolts from the Parrotts gouged holes in Pulaski's walls as they tore large sections of bricks loose. After a 30-hour bombardment, Olmstead hoisted a white flag and surrendered the bastion. Union artillery had fired more than 5,200 projectiles at

Bombardment of Fort Pulaski, Cockspur Island, Georgia

"Colonel, they will make it pretty warm for you here with shells, but they cannot breach your walls at that distance."

—General Robert E. Lee to Colonel Charles Olmstead,
garrison commander at Fort Pulaski

the fort, seriously damaging its walls and placing the interior powder magazines in jeopardy if struck. Remarkably, only one Confederate soldier was killed and a handful wounded during the intense bombardment.

Once captured, Fort Pulaski remained in Union hands throughout the war, effectively closing Savannah to blockade running. Rifled cannon projectiles could wear down and breach brick walls with relative ease, making these old forts obsolete.

FORT PULASKI

Did You Know?

Fort Pulaski became a prison when a group of Confederate soldiers were transferred there in 1864. These soldiers, called "The Immortal Six Hundred," were positioned in direct line of Confederate fire from Fort Sumter in response to news that six hundred Union soldiers were being held in the line of Union fire in Charleston, South Carolina. Thirteen prisoners died there, most of them from dehydration due to dysentery. The rest were transferred to Fort Delaware in Wilmington, Delaware, in March 1865.

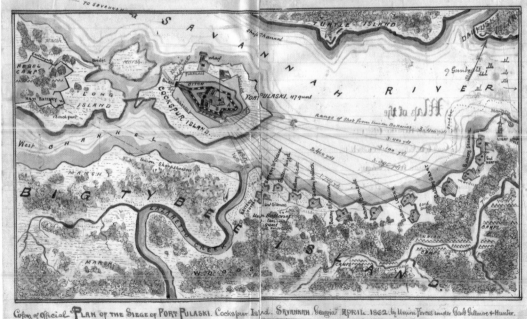

Official plan of the siege of Fort Pulaski

CIVIL WAR MONEY

During the Civil War, the Confederacy issued its own currency. The only facility that could produce coins for the Confederate government was the New Orleans branch of the U. S. Mint. When New Orleans was recaptured by the Union, only paper currency could be produced. More than 72 major types of Confederate notes were issued between 1861 and 1864, but all became worthless at the war's end.

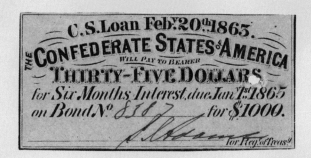

CIVIL WAR MEDALS

A navy version of the U.S. Medal of Honor was the first to be approved by President Lincoln in 1861. At the time, the Medal of Honor was the only decoration formally authorized by the United States government. An army version was approved the following year. The Confederate government, in an effort to increase morale, also authorized medals and badges for recognition of conduct during battle.

Union troops under Brigadier General Silas Casey's command built this earthen redoubt in May 1862. Attacking Confederate troops overran this position after heavy fighting during the Battle of Fair Oaks. The twin farmhouses in the background were a prominent feature on this part of the battlefield. (Today, this area is the site of a housing development.)

RICHMOND
BELEAGUERED CONFEDERATE CAPITAL

VISITOR INFORMATION

Name Richmond

Classification National Battlefield Park

Established March 2, 1936. Boundary change: March 3, 1956

Contact 3215 East Broad Street, Richmond, VA 23223

Phone 804-226-1981

Website www.nps.gov/rich

Acreage 7,307 (Federal: 773.03; Nonfederal: 6,533.97)

Points of Focus Beaver Dam Creek, Chickahominy Bluff, Cold Harbor, Drewry's Bluff, Fort Harrison, Gaines' Mill, Malvern Hill, Parker's Battery, Tredegar Iron Works, Watt House

Tours/Paths Self-guided walking tours, driving tour

Hours Visitor centers open daily from 9:00 a.m. to 5:00 p.m. Closed Thanksgiving, December 25, and January 1

Park Fee Free

Programs Orientation film, Junior Ranger program, several special events throughout the year

Facilities Five visitor centers, picnic area

When the Confederate government voted to move its capital to Richmond, Virginia, in May 1861, it meant that this city would become a focal point of contending armies. A hundred miles from Washington, Richmond was the state's major city and cultural center, situated at the head of navigation along the James River. The city also contained the Tredegar Iron Works, one of the South's largest such industries, as well as several other important businesses.

Major General George McClellan

Major General George B. McClellan, in command of the Union Army of the Potomac, planned a major campaign designed to capture the city and end the war in the spring of 1862. Rather than advance overland, his massive 120,000-man force landed at Fort Monroe, at the tip of the peninsula, then approached the Yorktown defenses. Here Confederate general John B. Magruder held off the Yankees until reinforced by General Joseph E. Johnston's entire army. But still outnumbered, Johnston elected to avoid McClellan's planned siege operations

RICHMOND NATIONAL BATTLEFIELD PARK ★ RICHMOND, VIRGINIA

THE GREAT ESCAPE

Situated in Richmond near the James River front, Libby Prison was an old tobacco warehouse that became a prison for Union officers. Terrible living conditions and overcrowding quickly made it one of the most notorious prisons in the Confederacy. Many men attempted escape; the largest of such efforts was led by Colonel Thomas E. Rose. Under the watchful eye of prison guards, it took a group of prisoners a mere 17 days to dig a 53-foot-long tunnel underneath the prisons, under a street, and into a backyard nearby. On February 9, 1886, 109 officers escaped through this tunnel; 59 reached Union lines, 2 drowned, and 48 were re-captured, including Colonel Rose. In 1888, a Chicago business purchased the building, dismantled it brick by brick, numbered every piece, and reassembled the old prison in Chicago. It then opened as a museum, closing a decade later. In 1899 it was torn down to make way for developers, and pieces of the prison were either discarded or sold.

Libby Prison

and withdrew, fighting a rearguard battle at Williamsburg on May 5. A Union naval squadron attempted to approach the capital city of Richmond via the James River, but on May 15 it was repelled by Confederate armaments located in Fort Darling at Drewry's Bluff.

McClellan then moved to within a few miles of Richmond, with his army on both sides of the flooded Chickahominy River. Johnston attacked the Union left at Fair Oaks (also called Seven Pines) on May 31–June 1, but after a sharp battle, Union reinforcements crossed the river and Johnston withdrew. The general himself was wounded in this battle; President Jefferson Davis replaced him with Robert E. Lee.

Subsequently Lee decided on an aggressive strategy that would drive the Yankees away from Richmond.

Siege trenches as they look today

Fighting at Oak Grove on June 25 near the old Fair Oaks battlefield was a diversion to mask Lee's major attacks north of the Chickahominy, where he was attempting to destroy one of McClellan's corps, Union general Fitz John Porter's Fifth Corps. Stonewall Jackson's troops traveled by rail from the Shenandoah Valley to reinforce Lee's Army of Northern Virginia. The first major engagement of the Seven Days Battles took place on June 25 when Lee's troops attacked Porter at Mechanicsville, also known as Beaver Dam Creek. Jackson failed to arrive on time and Porter's troops easily repelled Lee's frontal attacks. Porter fell back behind Boatswain's Swamp that night. Then followed the June 26 Battle of Gaines' Mill, where Porter's tired men repelled several enemy attacks. But by day's end, Longstreet and Jackson broke through and Porter fell back across the Chickahominy.

Porter's retreat influenced McClellan to change his supply base from White

Union Major General Fitz John Porter and his staff

Did You Know?

In the spring of 1862, Union General George B. McClellan led an army of 100,000 soldiers from Fort Monroe up the peninsula in an effort to capture Richmond, the capital city of the Confederacy, and end the war. This campaign—called The Seven Days Battles—was among the war's most critical series of engagements. After six major battles and several smaller ones, Robert E. Lee's army secured Richmond, paving the way for victories at Cedar Mountain and Manassas.

House on the Pamunkey River to Harrison's Landing on the James. His army destroyed what supplies it could not carry, abandoned several hospitals filled with sick and wounded men, and began a retreat toward the James River. Lee, hoping to catch McClellan's army, which was strung out in columns, hit the Pennsylvania Reserves division at Glendale on June 30. The fighting here (also known as Frayser's Farm and New Market Crossroads) was fierce, bloody, and obstinate, but the Pennsylvania troops, reinforced by the Third Corps, blunted General James Longstreet's assaults and allowed McClellan to take position on Malvern Hill. Lee attacked here on July 1, but massed Union artillery, supported by gunboats on the James, blasted charging Southern columns and repelled their attacks. The seven days cost McClellan 15,855 casualties. Lee's army suffered a loss of 20,204, but it had driven McClellan away from Richmond.

> "I have always regretted that the last assault at Cold Harbor was ever made. . . . At Cold Harbor no advantage whatever was gained to compensate for the heavy loss we sustained."
>
> —Union General Ulysses S. Grant

Subsequent Union raids directed against Richmond's growing defenses failed for the next two years. In May 1864, Lieutenant General Ulysses S. Grant directed George Meade's Army of the Potomac against Lee's army in a massive campaign that began in the Wilderness and wound up in siege operations at Petersburg in mid-June. After inconclusive battles at the Wilderness, Spotsylvania, and the North Anna, the two armies converged on the crossroads of Cold Harbor, situated on part of the old Gaines' Mill battlefield of two years before. Grant had continued to attempt to outflank all of Lee's positions ever since the campaign began, and the race to Cold Harbor echoed the Union general's earlier strategy.

Reinforced by 16,000 men from General Benjamin Butler's Army of the James, Grant directed Meade to seize the crossroads and attempt to outflank Lee yet again. Even though Union cavalry grabbed the crossroads on May 31 and reinforcing infantry from the Sixth Corps solidified their position, Lee's army sidled to the left and entrenched to face the Yankees. Lee, worried about being outflanked and knowing of Union reinforcements, wired to President Davis, expressing concern that if his own army was not augmented, he faced "disaster." Within hours, a fresh division from the Petersburg defenses moved to join Lee.

A Union frontal attack

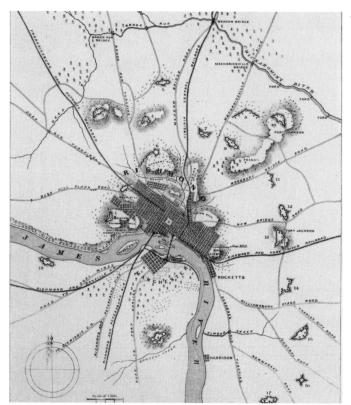

Richmond and its defenses

by the Sixth Corps was repelled on June 1, causing 2,200 Union casualties. Grant planned more assaults on June 2 and ordered General Winfield S. Hancock's Second Corps into position, but hot weather enervated the marching infantry and the attack was rescheduled for June 3. But three corps that assailed Lee's entrenched veterans that day were again repelled after some minor lodgements in the enemy fortifications. Grant's loss for the entire Battle of Cold Harbor totaled some 12,000 men. The general then decided to shift his troops across the James River to strike at Petersburg.

The subsequent siege operations around Petersburg occasionally involved troops that had been defending Richmond as well. Union operations on the north bank of the James centered around their bridgehead at Deep Bottom. Occasional forays against Richmond's defenses were primarily in an effort to

Battle of Cold Harbor

divert Lee's attention when Union troops maneuvered on the left of the line toward Petersburg's vital railroads.

One major operation took place in late September 1864. Troops from the Army of the James moved to the New Market Heights area to assault the Richmond defenses even as Union troops moved westward from the Petersburg siege lines on the other end of the Union positions. On September 29 Confederate Fort Harrison fell to a determined Yankee assault that included black troops; 14 African Americans later were awarded Medals of Honor for their gallantry in this attack. Later attacks against Fort Gilmer

ZOUAVES

Named for a Berber tribe from Algeria that fought for the French, Zouaves were infantry units that adopted the colorful garb of these French units—a short dark blue jacket with yellow or red trim, baggy trousers (red or blue), a woolen sash, white leggings, and a red fez for a cap, often with a turban as well. In 1859, Elmer Ellsworth organized the United States Zouave Cadets of Chicago; his tour across the north led many militia companies to adopt a flashy Zouave uniform. When the Civil War began, several entire regiments of men clothed in various Zouave-style uniforms appeared. Perhaps the best known was the 5th New York Infantry, known as Duryee's Zouaves after its first commander. During the Battle of Gaines' Mill, the 5th New York held the right of the Union line. The Zouaves encountered a brigade of South Carolinians and inflicted heavy casualties on it. But in return, the 5th lost a third of its 450 men, including 54 killed.

Zouave uniform of the 5th New York

"As the sun rose on Richmond, such a spectacle was presented as can never be forgotten by those who witnessed it. . . . All the horrors of the final conflagration, when the earth shall be wrapped in flames and melt with fervent heat, were, it seemed to us, prefigured in our capital. . . . [Then] a cry was raised: 'The Yankees! The Yankees are coming!'"

—Sallie Putnam

Position of Union troops in Richmond, Virginia, on May 27, 1862

failed, but Fort Harrison remained in Union hands, necessitating a realignment of the Richmond defenses to the north.

During the war, Richmond's population dramatically increased as refugees fled areas of fighting and moved into the city. The city also boasted the Confederacy's largest hospital (Chimborazo, location of the current park headquarters) and contained several POW camps, including Belle Island and Libby Prison. When Lee evacuated Petersburg on April 2, 1865, the Richmond garrison also retreated. Union troops marched into the city on April 3, helping to control fires set by retreating Rebels who burned military property.

Did You Know?

As the political and industrial capital of the Confederacy, Richmond, Virginia, was at the heart of the Civil War conflict. President Lincoln visited the city twice during the war: in July 1862, to meet with General George McClellan, who was attempting to capture Richmond in a series of battles, and on April 4, 1865, just two days after the Confederate army evacuated the city and shortly before Lee's surrender at Appomattox Court House. Richmond still smoldered with fire when Lincoln walked the streets with his son Tad, hoping to hasten the end of the bloody Civil War.

President Lincoln and his son Tad walk the streets of Richmond, the capital of the Confederacy, on April 4, 1865, just days after its capture by the Union army.

Name Antietam

Classification National Battlefield

Established Park—August 30, 1890. Transferred from War Department August 10, 1933; redesignated November 10, 1978. Boundary changes: May 14, 1940; April 22, 1960; May 31, 1963; November 10, 1978. Cemetery—Date of Civil War interments: 1866. Placed under War Department July 14, 1870. Transferred from War Department August 10, 1933

Contact P.O. Box 158, Sharpsburg, MD 21782

Phone 301-432-5124

Website www.nps.gov/ancm

Acreage 3,230 (Federal: 2,742; Nonfederal: 488)

Points of Focus Antietam National Cemetery, Burnside Bridge (Lower Bridge), the Cornfield, Dunker Church, Sunken Road

Tours/Paths 8.5-mile self-guided driving tour

Hours Labor Day to Memorial Day: 8:30 a.m. to 5:00 p.m.; Memorial Day to Labor Day: 8:30 a.m. to 6:00 p.m. Closed Thanksgiving, December 25, and January 1

Park Fee $4 per person ages 16 and up (3-day pass); free for visitors ages 15 and under. $6 per family; $20 annual pass; $80 Antietam partner pass. Group rates available

Programs 26-minute orientation film, 1-hour documentary, Ranger-led discussions (summer season only), Junior Ranger program, interpretive program

Facilities Visitor center, campsite, observation room, museum, theater, exhibits

ANTIETAM
AMERICA'S BLOODIEST DAY

Following his conquest of John Pope at the Battle of Second Manassas, General Robert E. Lee decided to launch an offensive into Maryland. He hoped to recruit sympathetic Marylanders into his army, ease the burden on northern Virginia farmers, and perhaps win a victory on Northern soil, an action that might lead to foreign recognition of the Confederacy.

General Lee's army of 40,000 men began crossing the Potomac River on September 4, 1862. A Federal garrison of 12,000 soldiers at Harper's Ferry threatened Lee's communications with Virginia. Seeing that recruits were not flocking to the Stars and Bars, Lee divided his army into four separate columns, sending three under the command of Stonewall Jackson to encircle and capture Harper's Ferry. Lee remained behind with General James Longstreet in Maryland, looking for supplies and watching the roads toward Washington.

In the meantime, General George B. McClellan reassumed command of the demoralized Union armies that had congregated in the Washington defense perimeter. McClellan used his

Signal tower overlooking Antietam battlefield

ANTIETAM NATIONAL BATTLEFIELD ★ SHARPSBURG, MARYLAND

This part of the famous Sunken Road at Antietam, now a peaceful farm lane, became a key battlefield point. Today, reconstructed wooden fences, closely mown grass, and stone monuments disguise the carnage that took place here.

CLARA BARTON

Clara Barton, a Massachusetts schoolteacher, was nicknamed "the angel of the battlefield" for her humanitarian work during the Civil War. Accompanied by four teamsters and a load of provisions, Barton arrived on the battlefield the day before the epic battle at Antietam. During the battle she extracted a bullet from a soldier's cheek, helped a surgeon with amputations, and passed out her own supplies to wounded men, all while in great danger. At one point, while kneeling to tend to a soldier, a bullet whizzed past her and killed the man she was helping.

After six weeks of hard work in the hospitals, Barton became sick and returned to Washington. She worked in army hospitals sporadically during the war, and in 1865 she helped identify unknown dead at Andersonville Prison. Barton later founded the American Red Cross and was its first director. She died in 1912 at the age of 91.

Clara Barton

genius for organization and quickly had the old Army of Virginia merged into his own Army of the Potomac. After leaving behind a substantial force to protect the capital, McClellan set out with about 80,000 men in five corps to confront Lee. Confederate cavalry quickly alerted Lee to McClellan's advance, so the outnumbered Confederates pulled out of Frederick and retreated to the passes through South Mountain west of the city.

McClellan's army moved into the Frederick area on September 13. That morning Union soldiers from the 27th Indiana regiment discovered Lee's General Orders Number 191, wrapped around three cigars. A staff officer must have carelessly dropped these orders, which were passed along to McClellan. Jubilant that he had Lee's battle plans, McClellan could scarcely believe his good luck.

McClellan's troops assailed the Rebel defenders of South Mountain on September 14. This engagement, known

Battle of Antietam, *published in 1863*

> ## "My ramrod is wrenched from my grasp as I am about to return it to its socket after loading. I look for it behind me, and the Lieutenant passes me another, pointing to my own, which lies bent and unfit for use across the face of a dead man."
>
> —*Private George Kimball, 12th Massachusetts, describing fighting in the Cornfield*

as the Battle of South Mountain, took place at Fox's and Turner's Gaps. By day's end, Union troops had driven off the defenders and were poised to relieve Harper's Ferry and also deliver a death-blow to Lee's army. But McClellan, fearing a trap, delayed his advance. As a result, Jackson seized the heights overlooking Harper's Ferry and began firing artillery into the Union lines. On September 15, Colonel Dixon S. Miles surrendered the entire garrison.

Lee retreated to the village of Sharpsburg, situated near the Potomac on a ridge overlooking Antietam Creek. Rather than retreat to Virginia, he decided to risk a battle, taking into account his adversary's usual cautious approach to fighting. Jackson's men joined Lee, even as McClellan's right wing crossed the creek and skirmished with Jackson's

troops on the evening of September 16.

The Battle of Antietam, called Sharpsburg by the Confederates, took place on September 17, which became the bloodiest day of the Civil War. McClellan outnumbered Lee by at least two to one, but instead of a concerted attack all along the line, the Union general allowed his subordinates to attack piecemeal, enabling the outnumbered Confederates to move reinforcements to threatened parts of their battle line throughout the day.

The first attacks took place shortly after dawn, when Union major general Joseph Hooker sent his First Corps into action against the Confederate left, held by troops under Jackson's command. A 30-acre cornfield then became the center of a fierce struggle between men in blue and gray. The fighting swept to and fro

HARPER'S FERRY

General Lee's invasion of Maryland in 1862 centered around the capture of the 12,000-man Union garrison at Harper's Ferry. Lee divided his army into four parts, sending Stonewall Jackson with three of these divisions to surround the garrison, which was under the command of Colonel Dixon S. Miles. Many of Miles's regiments were untested rookies. When Confederate troops pressured Union defensive positions, Miles evacuated the commanding Maryland Heights after only a brief engagement.

Discouraged when Confederate artillery batteries placed his men in a crossfire, Miles decided to surrender. However, Colonel Benjamin F. Davis gathered 1,300 cavalrymen, including his own 8th New York, crossed the Potomac River, and marched his horsemen along a little-used path under the very noses of Rebel sentinels to escape the trap. En route to safety, Davis happened upon General James Longstreet's reserve ammunition wagon train. His men seized and brought them as a prize into Union lines. Miles's surrender was the largest capitulation of American forces until Bataan in 1942. Miles himself was mortally wounded by an exploding shell and thus missed the court of inquiry and rebuke by the War Department over his handling of the situation.

THE YOUNGEST MEDAL OF HONOR WINNER

Bugler Johnny Cook of Battery B, 4th United States Artillery, had just turned 15 a month before going into action at Antietam. The battery unlimbered astride the Hagerstown Pike and immediately went into battle. Confederate musketry fire was heavy and the battery quickly sustained many casualties. Captain James Campbell was hit twice and his horse fell dead. Bugler Cook helped the captain to the rear and then returned to the action. He recalled: "Seeing that the cannoneers were nearly all down, and one with a pouch full of ammunition, lying dead, I unstrapped the pouch, started for the battery and worked as a cannoneer. We were then in the very vortex of battle. The enemy made three attempts to capture our guns, the last time coming within ten or fifteen feet of our guns." For his gallantry, Cook was awarded a Medal of Honor.

Johnny Cook

across this field as the two sides charged and countercharged through almost-ripe corn. By morning's end, the field was leveled and hundreds of bodies littered its surface.

Troops from General Joseph K.F. Mansfield's Twelfth Corps relieved the battered First Corps and continued the fight, sweeping through the East Woods, across the cornfield, and into the edges of the West Woods. A small, whitewashed church used by the Dunker sect became the Union target. The church sat on a small knoll a short distance south of the cornfield, its white walls a beacon for attacking Union soldiers. But the aged General Mansfield was hit in the stomach and carried from the field soon after his men became engaged, and his corps quickly became disorganized in the swirling combat.

General Edwin V. Sumner's Second

Cavalry marching out of Harper's Ferry

Corps then entered the fray. Sumner personally led the Second Division (led by General John Sedgwick) from Antietam Creek westward across the area of the earlier fighting into the West Woods, the men marching in three long brigade lines as if on dress parade. As the division reached the West Woods, Jackson's survivors struck from three sides; in less than 20 minutes, the Second Division disintegrated, suffering 2,300 casualties.

The rest of Sumner's corps drifted south and encountered Confederate troops under the command of D. H. Hill, arrayed in an old sunken farm lane. The Rebels repelled attack after attack until outflanked and forced to withdraw. But the defenders had mauled two Union divisions and held this portion of the line for four hours, against all odds, until flanked and driven back. Thereafter, the farm lane would be known as Bloody Lane. Conspicuous on the Union side was Thomas F. Meagher's Irish Brigade, composed largely of Irish immigrants from New York and Boston; in spite of heavy losses, they followed their green flags into the face of murderous enemy fire. As troops moved forward in this part of the field, a Confederate shell hit some beehives on the Roulette Farmstead. A passing Pennsylvania regiment dissolved as an entire swarm of maddened bees attacked the first objects they saw—these untried Keystone State boys broke ranks and fled to avoid the stinging.

On the southern end of the battlefield, Union general Ambrose E. Burnside was ordered to seize an arched stone bridge that spanned Antietam Creek and assail Lee's right flank. Burnside was slow in moving as he looked for a better place to cross the stream. Georgia troops occupied the heights overlooking the bridge, and their deadly fire broke up the first three Union charges against the bridge. Meanwhile, Burnside sent one of his divisions downstream to look for a ford. He also sent orders for another attack against the bridge, which came to be called Burnside's Bridge. At 1:00 p.m., two regiments charged the bridge. These men—the 51st Pennsylvania and 51st New York—reached the span together and managed to cross as the Georgians ran low on ammunition and withdrew. Burnside then crossed with his entire Ninth Corps,

Union soldiers and officers at Antietam, October 1862

occupied the hills overlooking the creek, reorganized, and later in the afternoon sent his entire corps forward against Lee's out-manned right flank. Even as Burnside's advance regiments reached the outskirts of Sharpsburg, troops from Ambrose P. Hill's division arrived from Harper's Ferry, racing to attack Burnside's left. This last Confederate division to reach the battlefield stemmed Burnside's advance and drove his corps back to the hills near the creek, where the blue line stabilized and held off the Confederates.

The fighting on the Union left effectively ended the day-long battle of Antietam. McClellan still had an entire corps in reserve, but the casualty rate for the day was appalling. His army had suffered 12,401 killed, wounded,

THE 23RD OHIO AT ANTIETAM

The 23rd Ohio Volunteer Infantry was mustered into Union service during the summer of 1861. After service in western Virginia, the regiment's division was transferred temporarily to the Ninth Corps and fought in the 1862 Maryland Campaign. The regiment's commander was Rutherford B. Hayes, a Harvard Law School graduate who volunteered early in the war to help stamp out the rebellion. Hayes was a fearless combat leader; at the Battle of South Mountain on September 14, the colonel was badly wounded in the arm and was out of action for months. The commissary sergeant of the 23rd was William McKinley, only 19 years old when he participated in the Battle of Antietam. He won plaudits for his bravery under fire, when he drove his commissary wagon through a rain of shot and shell from the enemy to bring badly needed food and coffee to the regiment in battle line.

Both Hayes and McKinley entered politics after the war and used their Civil War records to good effect. Both men became president of the United States. McKinley was the last veteran of the war to be elected president. In 1903, his old unit erected a monument to his heroism on the Antietam battlefield.

and captured. Many of his regiments had just joined the army and lacked effective training; their high losses contributed to the army's butcher's bill. Lee's smaller army suffered a loss of 10,318. McClellan refused to fight the next day, and on the evening of September 18, Lee quietly slipped across the Potomac. McClellan did not pursue Lee and instead went into camp near the battlefield, causing President Lincoln great frustration.

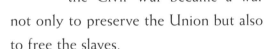

Lieutenant General Ambrose P. Hill

Even though Antietam was not a clear-cut Union victory, Abraham Lincoln used it to issue a preliminary draft of his Emancipation Proclamation. If the South did not lay down its arms and return to the Union by January 1, 1863, said the president, after that date all slaves held in rebellious states would be then and forever free. Thus the Civil War became a war not only to preserve the Union but also to free the slaves.

The Middle Bridge over Antietam Creek

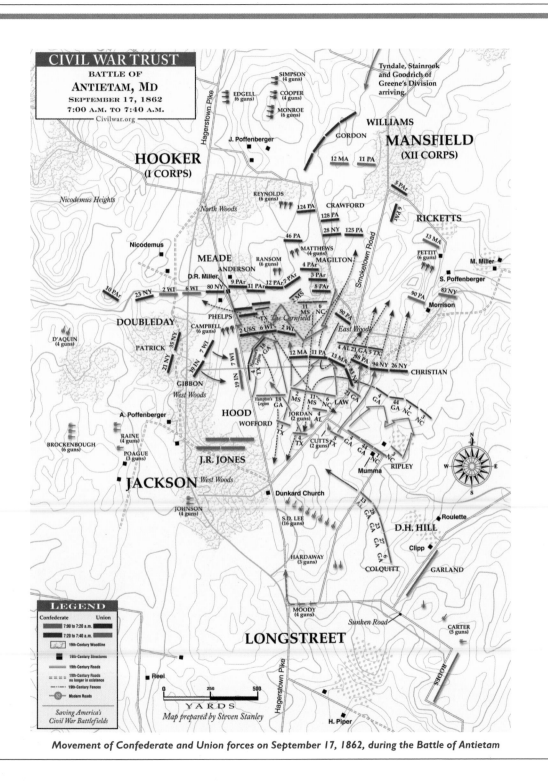

Movement of Confederate and Union forces on September 17, 1862, during the Battle of Antietam

"It was no longer alone the boom of the batteries, but a rattle of musketry— at first like pattering drops upon a roof; then a roll, crash, roar, and rush, like a mighty ocean billow upon the shore, chafing the pebbles, wave on wave, with deep and heavy explosions of the batteries, like the crashing of the thunderbolts."

—Army Correspondent Charles Carleton Coffin

ANTIETAM

Kurz & Allison's lithograph of Union troops surging across Burnside's Bridge

Union general Ambrose E. Burnside—commanding the Army of the Potomac from his position on Stafford Heights, northeast of the Rappahannock River—issues orders to Major General Joseph Hooker during the Battle of Fredericksburg, Virginia. Hooker protested his order to assail the Confederate position on Marye's Heights overlooking Fredericksburg.

FREDERICKSBURG

EPICENTER OF VIRGINIA'S CIVIL WAR

This military park embraces fields on which men in blue and gray fought four major battles of the war, with a combined casualty list of over 100,000 officers and men. The city of Fredericksburg, situated on the Rappahannock River, lies halfway between Richmond and Washington. Although the city had been occupied briefly by Union troops in May and June 1862, the war generally had been waged elsewhere until late November 1862, when both armies moved into the area.

Union major general Ambrose E. Burnside replaced George B. McClellan as commander of the Army of the Potomac in early November. The general devised a plan by which his massive army of more than 120,000 men would side-step Lee's Army of Northern Virginia and quickly move to Fredericksburg, where pontoon bridges would enable it to cross before Lee got there. Once across the river, Burnside would try to get between Lee and Richmond, thereby forcing a climactic battle.

But bureaucratic snafus delayed the pontoons' arrival from Washington, and by the time they arrived, Lee had guessed Burnside's maneuver and had reached the

Confederate statue at Fredericksburg

VISITOR INFORMATION

Name Fredericksburg & Spotsylvania

Classification National Military Park

Established Park—February 14, 1927. Transferred from War Department August 10, 1993. Boundary changes: December 11, 1989; October 27, 1992; December 9, 1999. Cemetery—Date of Civil War interments: 1867. Transferred from War Department August 10, 1933

Contact 120 Chatham Lane, Fredericksburg, VA 22405

Phone 540-373-6122

Website www.nps.gov/frsp

Acreage Park—8,535.02 (Federal: 7,369; Nonfederal: 1,166.02). Cemetery—12 (all Federal)

Points of Focus Chancellorsville, Chatham, Fredericksburg National Cemetery, Old Salem Church, Spotsylvania Court House, Stonewall Jackson Shrine

Tours/Paths 23 miles of walking, hiking, and biking trails; self-guided driving tour

Hours Open daily from 9:00 a.m. to 5:00 p.m. Closed Thanksgiving Day, December 25, and January 1

Park Fee $2 per person ages 10 to 61; $1 per person ages 62 and up

Programs Junior Ranger program, Ranger-led programs (summer season only)

Facilities Two visitor centers, picnic areas

General Ambrose E. Burnside

FREDERICKSBURG & SPOTSYLVANIA NATIONAL MILITARY PARK ★ FREDERICKSBURG, VIRGINIA

A CONFEDERATE'S HEROISM

During the bloody Union repulses at Fredericksburg's Marye's Heights, dozens of wounded men in blue lay in front of the enemy-occupied stone wall. Sergeant Richard Kirkland of the 2nd South Carolina was so moved by their desperate cries for help that he wanted to go over the wall and give them water. Against the better judgment of his commander, Kirkland collected canteens from several comrades and slowly stood up. He cautiously jumped over the wall and went to the nearest Union man. When it was seen that he was on an errand of mercy, nobody shot at him. Kirkland was allowed to administer to all the wounded within his range; then he returned to his post. Kirkland was killed in battle later in the war.

Confederate dead behind the stone wall of Marye's Heights, photographed in May 1863

hills behind Fredericksburg and deployed his army for battle. Burnside, feeling pressure from Washington to do something before winter set in, went ahead with his plan in spite of remonstrances from his subordinates. On December 11, engineers began laying the pontoons, but Rebel sniper fire from Fredericksburg stopped them cold. Union artillery then opened fire on the city as troops rowed across the river and fought the enemy in the streets until the city was secure. Then,

with the bridges completed, Burnside's army crossed.

THE BATTLE OF FREDERICKSBURG

The Battle of Fredericksburg took place on December 13. Burnside's plan called for an attack by his left wing, but Major General William B. Franklin, in charge of that wing, interpreted his orders too literally and sent forward only George Meade's Pennsylvania Reserves division. Meade's gallant soldiers broke through

Union troops build pontoon bridges across the Rappahannock River on December 12, 1862.

Stonewall Jackson's position at Hamilton's Crossing but were repelled when reinforcements failed to exploit this gain.

On the Union right, troops under Joseph Hooker and Edwin Sumner's command marched out of the city to assail Southern troops on Marye's Heights. Confederate troops sheltered by a stone wall and amply supported by artillery mowed down the Union attackers, who were unable to get close to the enemy. Lee, watching the slaughter, remarked, "It is well war is so terrible. We should grow too fond of it."

The following day was spent in skirmishing as Burnside debated what to do. But that night, his army silently recrossed the river and went into winter quarters. Casualties totaled 12,653 Federals and only 5,309 Confederates. Fredericksburg was Lee's most lopsided victory of the war.

After the battle, recriminations on the Union side led to Burnside's dismissal and his replacement by Major General Joseph Hooker. Hooker instituted much-needed changes to bolster the shattered morale

Lithograph by Henry Alexander Ogden depicting General Robert E. Lee surveying the fighting on the first day at Fredericksburg

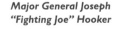

Major General Joseph "Fighting Joe" Hooker

of his army. By the spring of 1863, the Army of the Potomac was, according to its commander, "the finest army on the planet." Hooker's plans called for a portion of his army to move northwest along the Rappahannock, then quickly cross both this river and the smaller Rapidan. This would enable his troops to move through an area called the Wilderness because of its largely wooded terrain, and approach Lee's rear flank. The rest of the army would confront Lee at Fredericksburg and prevent him from sending troops to

> "General, we cover that ground now so well that we will comb it as with a fine-tooth comb. A chicken could not live on that field when we open on it."
>
> —Artillery General E. P. Alexander to General Robert E. Lee

Union Major General Philip Kearney's men, injured during the Battle of Fredericksburg

oppose the flanking maneuver. Union cavalry would conduct a raid far to the rear to intercept Lee's communications. If all went well, Hooker boasted, Lee would either have to come out of his fortifications to fight, or retreat to Richmond.

FIGHTING AT CHANCELLORSVILLE

The campaign began on April 13, 1863, when Union horsemen departed on their

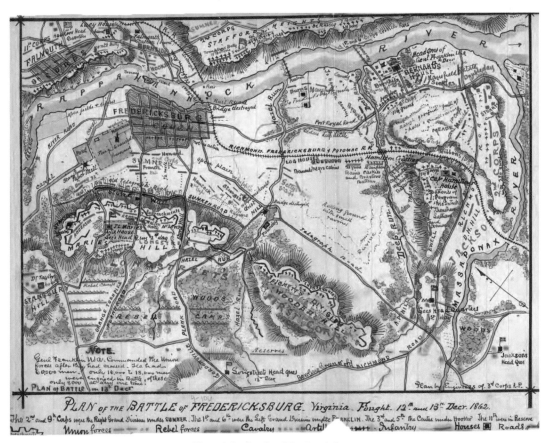

Plan of the Battle of Fredericksburg

raid. Rainy weather hampered their effectiveness, and it was not until April 27 that Hooker and three of his seven infantry corps began the flanking movement. By nightfall on April 30, these corps were grouped around a mansion called Chancellorsville, situated in cleared land in the midst of the Wilderness, less than 20 miles west of Fredericksburg. An elated Hooker called for the Third and most of the Second Corps to join him, giving him a clear superiority over Lee's depleted army; Lee had sent General Longstreet with part of his corps to the Suffolk region to guard against Union raids and gather supplies, and Longstreet was still absent.

General Thomas Jonathan "Stonewall" Jackson

Lee nevertheless had fathomed Hooker's intentions and sent his divisions west to confront the Union general. When skirmishing erupted on the morning of May 1, Hooker, instead of sending his troops forward until they cleared the Wilderness, pulled his divisions back into a defensive position to await Lee's attack. Later that day Southern cavalry discovered that Hooker's right flank was unguarded. Reacting to this news, Lee and Stonewall Jackson took a gamble. Jackson took three divisions (28,000 men), circled around to Hooker's right and attacked, leaving Lee with two divisions to oppose any sudden advance. A single division still occupied the Fredericksburg positions.

Jackson's flank march took place on May 2, and even though Yankee skirmishers located the route of march and General Daniel Sickles sallied forth with the Third Corps to see what was going on, General Oliver O. Howard, commanding the Eleventh Corps on Hooker's right, failed to take any precautions against attack. Thus, when Jackson's troops charged forth shortly after 6:00 p.m., Howard's corps was routed and Sickles, hastily recalled, had to conduct a night battle to link up with the main line. That night, while reconnoitering in front of his troops, Jackson was badly wounded by his own men, who mistakenly thought they were being attacked by enemy horsemen.

FREDERICKSBURG

BATTLEFIELD PRESERVATION

The roots of Civil War battlefield preservation go back to 1864, when Pennsylvania chartered a private corporation to preserve portions of the Gettysburg battleground. Other private groups emerged, but in the 1890s the federal government acquired the Gettysburg, Antietam, Shiloh, Chickamauga, and Vicksburg battle sites. Other parks were created through the years and in 1933 were turned over to the National Park Service for administration. The 1960s centennial, a concurrent rise in tourism, and developmental expansion threats to many battlefields led to an increase in preservation activism. Arkansas political consultant Jerry Russell formed the Civil War Round Table Associates in the late 1960s to warn the public of commercial and residential threats to sacred ground. By the 1980s, other organizations had formed in response to the lack of federal money for preservation. In 1988 and 1994, threats to Manassas, Virginia, garnered national headlines as proponents of preservation turned aside commercial threats to this site's integrity. Some sites, such as Chantilly in Virginia and those around Atlanta, have been lost to urbanization, but an increased awareness of cultural heritage has led to other victories in the quest to preserve the battlefields of the 1860s.

MUSIC UNDER FIRE

On May 6, 1864, the 45th Pennsylvania was one of many Union regiments to assail the Rebels in the tangled hell of the Wilderness. The 45th reached the enemy breastworks and planted its flag, but was forced to retreat. Captain Rees G. Richards was attempting to rally his company when he found Colonel John I. Curtin, distraught over the absence of the regimental flag. But soon, the color-bearer emerged through the acrid smoke, still carrying his bullet-ridden silk banner. Captain Richards, elated, seized the flag from the bearer and began to sing, "Rally round the flag, boys!/ Rally once again!/ Shouting the battle cry of freedom."

Other soldiers heard the captain and joined in. Soon, the entire regiment rallied as men hurried back into line, emboldened by the captain's singing. This incident, although seemingly trivial, shows how important a battle flag was to those who served beneath its folds. But these big infantry flags (in the Union army, 6 x 6½ feet in size) were ready-made targets for enemy fire. Color-bearers were slain by the score in large battles, and many Medals of Honor earned during the war were for actions involved in either saving or capturing flags.

Captain Rees G. Richards

May 3 saw desperate fighting around the Chancellor House as Hooker began to pull his army back into a tighter perimeter guarding the fords across the Rappahannock. The general himself was stunned when a shell struck a pillar on the Chancellor House porch, and even though subordinates wanted to counter-attack the disorganized Confederates, Hooker was adamant about retreating. In the meantime, Union general John Sedgwick's Sixth Corps attacked at Fredericksburg, broke through the thinly manned defenses, and headed for Chancellorsville. Lee sent troops to oppose Sedgwick, and the two forces engaged in combat at Salem Church before Sedgwick retreated and recrossed the Rappahannock on May 4.

Hooker's main army retreated to its old camps opposite Fredericksburg on May 6. His army lost 17,287 soldiers, while Lee's army counted 12,821 casualties. Stonewall Jackson's wounded arm

Kurz & Allison lithograph of the Battle of Chancellorsville

was amputated and the general was healing well until pneumonia set in; he died in a small house near Guinea Station on May 10. General Lee said that he "lost [his] right arm" when Jackson died.

The area next saw fighting a year later, in May 1864. Lieutenant General Ulysses S. Grant, in charge of all the Union armies, directed General Meade's Army of the Potomac, supported by General Burnside's Ninth Corps, to cross the Rapidan from its camps near Brandy Station and move through the Wilderness toward Fredericksburg. Grant felt that the army could move rapidly and reach clear terrain before Lee could engage the troops in battle. Even if the Confederate troops reached them, Grant felt that his 115,000 men would be able to handle Lee's much smaller army.

Cavalry detected the Union advance and Lee moved from his camps south of the Rapidan to the east to confront the Yankees. Fighting erupted on May 5 as troops from the two armies collided on the Orange Turnpike. Here,

General Winfield Hancock

two Union corps (the Fifth and Sixth) confronted Richard S. Ewell's corps from Lee's army. Farther south, General Winfield S. Hancock's Second Corps encountered troops from Ambrose P. Hill's Third Corps of Lee's army. By nightfall, battle lines were drawn and Lee awaited Longstreet's arrival from southwestern Virginia.

Fighting continued on May 5 as Hancock launched a massive attack that drove Hill back, but Longstreet's opportune arrival blunted the Yankees and forced a stalemate. Elsewhere, troops fighting in the tangled underbrush also had to contend with forest fires that threatened both sides and endangered the thousands of wounded men lying on the ground. The two days of fierce fighting cost Grant more than 18,000 men, with Lee's loss estimated at more than 8,000. However, instead of retreating, Grant ordered George Meade to move the army east, out of the Wilderness, heading around Lee's right flank.

Lee was forced to react and stay

"On the whole I think this plan was decidedly the best strategy conceived in any of the campaigns ever set foot against us. And the execution of it was, also, excellently managed, up to the morning of May 1st."

—Confederate artillery officer Edward Porter Alexander

BLOODY ANGLE'S OAK TREE

During the intense fighting at Spotsylvania on May 12, 1864, a sizeable oak tree between the lines eventually fell after being chipped away by bullet after bullet. The tree's demise was witnessed by hundreds of men who wrote about it in letters home or in postwar recollections. In May 1865, Union soldiers returning to Washington camped in the area and visited the site. Relic hunters quickly decimated the remains, and the oak stump had disappeared. General Nelson A. Miles traced it to a local innkeeper, who was persuaded to part with the souvenir. Miles presented the relic to Secretary of War Edwin M. Stanton. The stump is now in the collection of the Smithsonian Institution's National Museum of American History.

The oak stump

Going into Action by W. H. Shelton, showing cavalry and horse artillery troops at Chancellorsville

between Grant and the roads to Richmond. The two armies edged to the east and a series of battles took place between May 8 and 18, collectively called the Battle of Spotsylvania, named for the tiny village that served as the seat of Spotsylvania County. Confederate infantry from Longstreet's corps (now led by Richard H. Anderson after Longstreet's accidental wounding in the Wilderness) raced ahead to secure the crossroads, barely arriving before Union infantry began attacking on the afternoon of May 8 in an engagement sometimes called Laurel Hill. Lee's troops arrived and erected earthworks in

the shape of a large inverted "U" as the Yankees took positions nearby.

Union attacks continued on May 10 but were mostly repulsed. At 6:00 p.m., Colonel Emory Upton led 12 regiments in a bayonet charge against the western face of the Southern salient. Although Upton's charge broke into the enemy line, his outnumbered men were eventually forced back. But the attack gave Grant the idea to launch a much larger charge, this time using Hancock's entire Second Corps. This massive attack occurred as dawn broke on May 12. Rain soon set in, and although Hancock's initial charge shattered a Confederate division and seized several artillery batteries, it lost momentum as units became disorganized and Southern troops rushed to fill the breach. The rest of the day saw one of the most savage conflicts of the war as troops engaged in bloody hand-to-hand combat, at times separated only by log breastworks. After dark, when the Rebels had constructed a new defensive line at the base of the salient, they fell back and the 20-hour-long battle sputtered to a close.

The two armies remained in position for another week. Grant ordered an attack on May 18, but many regiments went into the battle only half-heartedly before retreating from the formidable enemy earthworks. The general then decided to move the army to the east again, forcing Lee to abandon his strong position. On May 19, Southern units probing the Union right flank encountered newly arrived regiments of heavy artillery from the Washington defenses. These artillerists had been given infantry equipment and sent to reinforce Grant. Although suffering severe casualties, these "heavies" slowed Ewell's attack long enough to enable reinforcements to arrive. Ewell then withdrew, and the fighting in the area was over as the armies headed south toward the North Anna River. Grant's army had lost more than 18,000 soldiers in the fighting at Spotsylvania, while Lee's casualties, although not reported as precisely, were at least 10,000. Grant was able to replace his losses, while Lee had difficulty finding reinforcements as his army dwindled in strength.

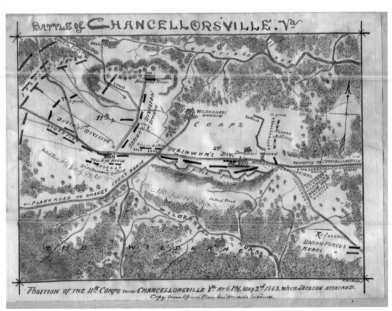

Map of the Battle of Chancellorsville

Did You Know?

General Lee's greatest victory was at Chancellorsville, but it came at a great cost. The Confederate army did not gain any ground, his army failed to achieve its objective (destroying the Union army), and while his troops had fewer casualties, he lost a higher overall percentage of his men. In addition, one of the Confederate army's greatest generals, Thomas Jonathan "Stonewall" Jackson, had been killed in friendly fire, creating a vacancy in leadership that would not be filled for the rest of the war.

Attack on Fredericksburg was created in 1862 by Alonzo Chappel. The drawing depicts Union troops landing on the shore of the Rappahannock River. Many arrive in boats, while others build pontoon bridges. As the Union soldiers advance toward the town, buildings burn in the background.

VISITOR INFORMATION

Name Stones River

Classification National Battlefield

Established Park—March 3, 1927. Transferred from War Department August 10, 1933; redesignated April 22, 1960. Boundary changes: April 22, 1960; December 23, 1987; December 11, 1991. Cemetery—Date of Civil War interments: 1865. Transferred from War Department August 10, 1933

Contact 3501 Old Nashville Highway, Murfreesboro, TN 37129

Phone 615-893-9501

Website www.nps.gov/stri

Acreage Park—708.32 (Federal: 494.10; Nonfederal: 214.13). Cemetery—20.09 (all Federal)

Points of Focus The Cotton Field, Defense of the Nashville Pike (Six-gun Chicago Board of Trade Battery), Fortress Rosecrans, Hazen Monument (Fight for the Round Forest), McFadden's Ford, The Slaughter Pen, Stones River National Cemetery

Tours/Paths Walking trails, self-guided driving tour

Hours Open daily from 8:00 a.m. to 5:00 p.m. Closed Thanksgiving Day and December 25

Park Fee Free

Programs Ranger-led walks and discussions (May to November), audiovisual orientation program, interpretive program

Facilities Visitor center, museum, recreation greenways

Following the unsuccessful Confederate invasion of Kentucky in October 1862 the Union Army of the Cumberland received a new commander, Major General William S. Rosecrans, an Ohio-born officer with previous successes in western Virginia and Mississippi. The new commander moved his army back to Nashville and divided it into three corps, led by generals George H. Thomas, Alexander M. McCook, and Thomas L. Crittenden.

Rosecrans's intrepid opponent was General Braxton Bragg and his Army of Tennessee, encamped near Murfreesboro, about 30 miles southeast of Nashville. Bragg's two corps commanders were generals Leonidas Polk and William J. Hardee. His 38,000 troops were outnumbered by Rosecrans's 44,000.

Goaded by the Lincoln administration to take some kind of action, Rosecrans finally began moving south on December 26, after beefing up his supply base at Nashville. By December 30, the Yankees had moved to within 2 miles of Murfreesboro, but a heavy rainstorm stalled

The Hazen Brigade Monument, erected at Stones River in 1863, is the oldest intact Civil War monument still in its original location.

The massed fire of 58 union guns like this smoothbore Napoleon cannon played a decisive role in repulsing the final Confederate attempt to recross Stones River after Union troops abandoned their defense of the Round Forest. The Confederates lost 1,700 of the 4,500 men who took part in the final attack.

"Many of the Yanks were either killed or retreated in their nightclothes. . . . We found a caisson with the horses still attached lodged against a tree and other evidences of their confusion. The Yanks tried to make a stand whenever they could find shelter of any kind. All along our route we captured prisoners, who would take refuge behind houses, fences, logs, cedar bushes and in ravines."

—Confederate Lieutenant Tunnel, 14th Texas Infantry

An idealized version of the Battle of Stones River in a Currier & Ives lithograph

their southward advance. Bragg concentrated his troops to oppose Rosecrans as the two armies drew near each other.

Instead of passively awaiting the Yankee attack, Bragg decided to launch a December 31 early-morning attack against the Union right flank. If all went according to plan, Hardee's troops would roll up the Union flank and drive the enemy back against the rain-swollen Stones River, which bisected Bragg's chosen battleground. But unbeknownst to Bragg, Rosecrans had decided on a similar maneuver. His left flank would strike Bragg's right and drive the Rebels away from Murfreesboro. The Yankee attack was likewise planned to start on December 31.

Bragg struck first. At dawn on the last day of 1862, Hardee's divisions charged

Major General William S. Rosecrans

> **"Men fell around on every side like autumn leaves and every foot of soil over which we passed seemed dyed with the life blood of some one or more of the gallant spirits whom I had the honor to command."**
>
> —Lieutenant Colonel J. J. Scales, 30th Mississippi

The Battle of Stones River or Murfreesboro by Union soldier A. E. Mathews, 31st Regiment

MUTINY

In late summer 1862, Captain William J. Palmer began recruiting the 15th Pennsylvania Cavalry. Nicknamed the "Anderson Cavalry," Palmer's unit was intended to act as headquarters guard for General Robert Anderson, the hero of Fort Sumter. The unit began recruiting at Carlisle, Pennsylvania. Palmer was captured while scouting during the Antietam operations and the regiment was sent to Nashville. Although it lacked proper officers, the regiment was ordered to help the advance of Murfreesboro. But the men mutinied, saying they had enlisted only to act as headquarters guards. Still, majors Adolph Rosengarten and Frank Ward took 300 of the mutineers into action on December 29, heading the advance toward the enemy. The regiment encountered infantry and was repulsed; both majors were killed. The remaining 600 men were thrown in prison until General Rosecrans worked out a deal to get the regiment back to work. Palmer was exchanged in February 1863 and reorganized his regiment, but the mutiny attached a stigma to the 15th that was never completely erased.

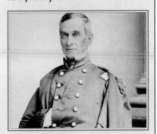

General Robert Anderson

CHAPLAIN JOHN M. WHITEHEAD

During the Civil War, fifteen Union army chaplains were killed or mortally wounded and four received Congressional Medals of Honor. One of these four was Chaplain John M. Whitehead of the 15th Indiana. During the fighting at Stones River, Whitehead, a Baptist minister, displayed great bravery in helping carry wounded men from the battle line as well as comforting dying men of his unit, which suffered heavy casualties. Captain Joel Foster, a peacetime neighbor from Westville, Indiana, fell mortally wounded into Whitehead's arms during the intense fighting in "Hell's Half Acre." Lieutenant Colonel Isaac Suman of the 9th Indiana was shot twice; Whitehead found the badly wounded officer and managed to extract a lead bullet from his side, then stanched the flow of blood from both wounds. "When Chaplain Whitehead gave me his assistance," recalled Suman, "he was all besmeared with the blood of the wounded he had cared for. He seemed to be an angel among the wounded, Yankees and Johnnies alike."

Chaplain John M. Whitehead

and hit the Yankee right flank, shattering the first Federal units they encountered. Richard Johnson's and Jefferson C. Davis's divisions were driven back toward Stones River by Hardee's troops. But Philip Sheridan's division of McCook's corps, although driven back, rallied and took position in the cedar woods around the Wilkinson Pike and held firm.

Rosecrans hurried reinforcements into the widening battle and by afternoon, Rebel attacks slowed against mounting numbers of Yankees and on account of their own disorganization. Soldiers dubbed one section of an area along the tracks of the Nashville & Chattanooga Railroad line "Hell's Half Acre" because of the intense close combat there. By

Kurz & Allison print of the Battle of Stones River

evening, the Southerners had withdrawn and reformed.

Bragg expected that Rosecrans would withdraw because his army was in a precarious position, with its back to Stones River. But the Union general merely straightened his line and remained on the field, daring Bragg to resume the contest. Rosecrans even established a new position on the opposite side of the river that would enable his artillery to enfilade any attacking columns.

Angered by his enemy's unwillingness to retreat, Bragg sent Brigadier General John C. Breckinridge's division across the river to capture the new enemy line. Breckinridge protested but launched his brigades into action late on the afternoon of January 2, 1863. Although suffering some loss, his troops drove the enemy from a low ridge and toward the river. But Major John Mendenhall, a Union artillery commander, had deployed 57 cannons across the stream in anticipation of such an emergency. His gunners blasted Breckinridge's troops as Yankee reinforcements splashed across the stream to recapture the ridge. After losing 1,700 men in less than an hour, Breckinridge, lacking reinforcements, fell back to his initial position.

The two armies again spent a cold, restless night sleeping on their weapons in anticipation of more action. On January 3, heeding the advice of his generals, Bragg decided to withdraw. His army had lost a total of 9,870 officers and men killed, wounded, and captured, a casualty rate of 26 percent. Rosecrans's casualty list totaled some 12,706 officers and men, 29 percent of his effective strength on the battlefield. Both sides claimed victory, but by withdrawing, Bragg conceded the field to Rosecrans, who did not pursue because of his own casualties and a postbattle heavy rain. The Union victory at Stones River provided welcome news to Northerners who had read of defeats at Fredericksburg, Virginia, and Grant's initial failure in his operations at Vicksburg, Mississippi.

Did You Know?

Prior to the Battle of Stones River, Union Major General William Rosecrans received a telegraph that stated: "The Government demands action, and if you cannot respond to that demand some one else will be tried." By urging Rosecrans into action, the U.S. government hoped to boost the morale of Union soldiers after the army's terrible defeat a few weeks earlier at Fredericksburg. The U.S. government also aimed to drum up support for the Emancipation Proclamation, which would go into effect on January 1, 1863.

CIVIL WAR PORTRAITS

Union Brigadier General Clinton Dugald MacDougall and staff

Union General Phil Sheridan and staff, January 3, 1865

Union Major General Silas Casey and staff

Union General M. D. Leggett and staff

The Civil War was the first large and prolonged conflict recorded by photography. Both the Confederate and Union governments employed photographers for formal portraits and to document the locations and aftermaths of battles. Because of the photographic technology of the time, action photographs during battles were not possible.

Union General John Buford and staff

Union General William Belknap and staff

Union General Henry Warner Slocum and staff

Union General James McMillan and staff

A part of the Wisconsin State memorial at Vicksburg, shown here on a hazy, gray day. The memorial commemorates the sacrifices of over 9,000 soldiers from that state who fought here in 1862–63.

VICKSBURG

UNVEXED TO THE SEA

VISITOR INFORMATION

Name Vicksburg

Classification National Military Park

Established Park—February 21, 1899. Transferred from War Department August 10, 1933. Boundary changes: June 4, 1963; October 18, 1990. Cemetery—Date of Civil War interments: 1866–74. Transferred from War Department August 10, 1933. Boundary change: March 2, 1955

Contact 3201 Clay Street, Vicksburg, MS 39183

Phone 601-636-0583

Website www.nps.gov/vick

Acreage 1,852.75

Points of Focus Battery Selfridge, Battery De Golyer, Fort Hill, Fort Garrott, Great Redoubt, Hovey's Approach, Railroad Redoubt, Ransom's Gun Path, Second Texas Lunette, Shirley House, Stockade Redan Attack, Stockade Redan, Thayer's Approach, Third Louisiana Redan, Vicksburg National Cemetery, USS *Cairo*

Tours/Paths 16-mile self-guided driving tour

Hours Visitor center open daily from 8:00 a.m. to 5:00 p.m. Closed December 25

Park Fee $4 per person; $8 per vehicle; $4 per person with bus/church van; $20 annual pass; $80 America the Beautiful pass

Programs USS *Cairo* film at USS *Cairo* Museum, audiovisual orientation film at visitor center, Living History program (summer season only)

Facilities Visitor center, USS *Cairo* Museum, picnic areas, bookstore

Considered by many historians to be the turning point of the Civil War, the campaign for Vicksburg, Mississippi, lasted from November 1862 until its surrender on July 4, 1863. General Ulysses S. Grant, in command of the Union Army of the Tennessee, was pitted against General John C. Pemberton, the Confederate general tasked with protecting Mississippi from invasion.

Vicksburg was situated on a high bluff overlooking a sharp bend in the Mississippi River. Its fortifications, which included several cannon batteries, controlled ship traffic on the river below. Seizing Vicksburg would go a long way in severing the Trans-Mississippi states from the rest of the Confederacy, as well as providing a water route for commodities to reach foreign markets from the Midwest.

Grant began his campaign from northern Mississippi in November 1862, intending to march overland to attack the city from the rear. But Confederate cavalry led by Earl Van Dorn raided Grant's supply base at Holly Springs, forcing Grant to retreat. General William T. Sherman, in

Lithograph of Ulysses S. Grant, surrounded by his major battles

VICKSBURG NATIONAL MILITARY PARK ★ VICKSBURG, MISSISSIPPI

THE USS *CAIRO*

This river ironclad, one of seven nicknamed "Pook's Turtles" after their designer, were in essence armored rafts with a shallow draft that enabled them to operate on the Mississippi River and its tributaries. The *Cairo* was 175 feet long, powered by a stern paddlewheel, and mounted 13 cannons. The ship's heavy armor limited her to a mere 5 knots. She was engaged in battle at Fort Pillow and Memphis, Tennessee, before steaming south to assist in the reduction of Vicksburg. In December 1862, the *Cairo* became the first warship to be sunk by an electrically detonated torpedo when she steamed over two enemy torpedoes positioned in the Yazoo River north of Vicksburg. The ship sank upright in 36 feet of water with no casualties. Rediscovered, the *Cairo* was raised in 1965 and after extensive conservation, was placed on display in the Vicksburg National Military Park in 1977.

The USS Cairo

command of one of Grant's wings, had gone down the Mississippi by boat and landed his troops just above the city, but his December 29 attack at Chickasaw Bluffs was repelled. Grant then marched to join Sherman at the new base of Milliken's Bend, upriver and on the opposite side from Vicksburg.

Grant had about 35,000 men available for duty after leaving behind enough troops to protect Memphis and other points in the rear. Throughout the winter of 1862–63, Grant sent expeditions into the bayous west of the Mississippi in a vain effort to find an alternative route around Vicksburg's defenses. One such attempt included digging a canal across the base of the peninsula opposite

Vicksburg and diverting the river channel, but high water flooded the canal before it was finished.

After these efforts failed, Grant decided to move his army downriver and try to cross below Vicksburg. Sherman's corps remained behind as a diversion while Grant's other two corps, led by generals James B. McPherson and John A. McClernand, began the strenuous task of filtering through the bayous. To further distract Pemberton, Grant sent Colonel Benjamin H. Grierson's cavalry on a raid through central Mississippi, wrecking telegraph lines, tearing up railroads, and forcing Pemberton's cavalry to chase him. Grierson's cavalry eventually reached Union lines at Baton Rouge after accomplishing their task.

On April 16, 1863, Union admiral David D. Porter's fleet steamed past the Vicksburg batteries, suffering minor damage. Porter's gunboats protected several troop transports sent to ferry Grant's troops across the river. Two weeks later a local contraband slave told Grant about a crossing place at Bruinsburg. Grant crossed there as Sherman's men marched to join the other two corps. On May 1,

The Union assault on May 22, 1863

JOHN C. PEMBERTON

Despite his lack of battlefield experience, John C. Pemberton was promoted to lieutenant general and sent to defend Vicksburg in 1862. There he had initial success in the field, fending off Union forces until spring 1863, when two bloody defeats drove him back into the city to endure the 47-day siege. Pemberton, called a traitor in the South for surrendering Vicksburg (the general was originally from Philadelphia but had married a Virginia woman), asked for a court of inquiry but never received a hearing. He resigned his general's commission and was reappointed a lieutenant colonel of artillery in the spring of 1864, serving initially in the defenses of Richmond.

After the war, Pemberton farmed in Virginia before returning to Philadelphia. His citizenship was restored in 1879. Pemberton died in 1881 and is buried in Philadelphia's Laurel Hill Cemetery. He wrote a memoir that defended his actions during the war, but it was only recently discovered and was not published until 1999.

McClernand and McPherson attacked Confederate troops led by General John S. Bowen, whose men blocked roads leading to Port Gibson. After a sharp engagement, Bowen was forced to retreat to Grand Gulf.

Grant then decided to march inland rather than doing the expected—move north directly upon Vicksburg. The general felt that he needed to disperse any Southern troops nearby and to try to isolate Pemberton's large garrison. Accordingly, Grant's army headed northeast. McPherson's corps encountered a lone Rebel brigade, commanded by John Gregg, at the village of Raymond on May 12. McPherson's men drove Gregg away and continued on toward Jackson, the state capital. Here, General Joseph E. Johnston had begun to gather troops to support Pemberton. But Johnston had only about 6,000 men, and when Grant

John C. Pemberton

Did You Know?

Both presidents, Abraham Lincoln and Jefferson Davis, understood that Vicksburg was the crucial key to winning the war. At the time, the Mississippi River, where Vicksburg was located, was the most important economic feature of North America. Lincoln stated, "The war can never be brought to a close until that key is in our pocket. . . . We can take all the Northern ports of the Confederacy, and they can defy us from Vicksburg."

attacked on May 14, Johnston delayed long enough to evacuate the city and retreat to the north. The Yankees occupied Jackson briefly, wrecking railroads and burning industries before heading west toward Vicksburg.

McPherson and McClernand encountered Pemberton with 22,000 men at Champion's Hill. This May 16 battle was the largest of the campaign. Superior Union numbers pushed the enemy off the field. Pemberton suffered 3,624 casualties, and one of his divisions was largely cut off during the retreat and marched to join Johnston. Grant struck again on the seventeenth at the Big Black River, launching a devastating attack that inflicted 1,024 casualties—mostly captured—on Pemberton's rearguard.

Pemberton withdrew into Vicksburg's formidable defenses. Grant, believing that his adversary was demoralized, attacked on May 19. However, his assaults were repelled with a loss of 942 men. Undeterred, Grant authorized another attack on May 22. He wanted to avoid a siege because of the menace of Johnston's growing army at his rear. Accordingly, his men assaulted on a front of 3 miles. Heavy fighting surged around

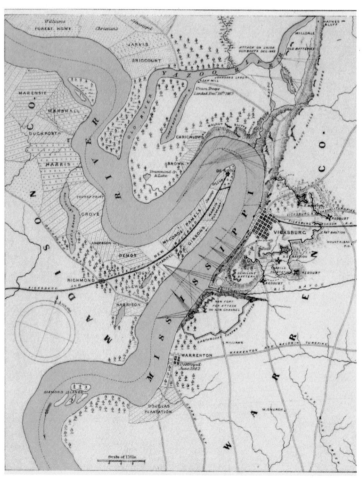

Vicksburg and its defenses

Confederate earthworks such as the Stockade Redan, the Great Redoubt, and the Railroad Redoubt. At this last place, Yankee soldiers swarmed in and drove off its defenders, but Texas troops counterattacked, and after a melee involving clubbed muskets, hand grenades, and bayonets, drove out the bluecoats. Union losses totaled 3,199.

Grant then extended his line and put the city and its garrison under siege. By the end of June, Grant's army had grown to 75,000 men. Porter's gunboats kept the city under fire and provided crews to man some of the Union siege batteries. Union troops began digging zigzag approach trenches to get closer to the Southern lines, but sharpshooters and the use of hand grenades made the going slow. Union soldiers also dug tunnels and exploded mines under two Confederate forts, but neither explosion helped rupture the enemy lines.

By late June, the state of affairs within Vicksburg was growing desperate. Food was rapidly disappearing, the city newspaper resorted to using wallpaper to print its last issues, and many citizens dug caves in order to escape the incessant shelling that was reducing the city to rubble. Pemberton wanted to break out of the city and join Johnston, but with more than 10,000 men on the sick lists, and a shortage of rations, it meant his forces were too weak for active operations.

So, on July 3, Pemberton raised a flag of truce and sought an audience with Grant. After some brief negotiating, Pemberton decided to surrender his 29,000 men on the condition that they would be paroled and sent home to await proper exchange as prisoners of war. The formal surrender took place on July 4. Grant then sent Sherman east against Johnston, who again evacuated Jackson after holding off the Yankees for a few days. When Port Hudson, Louisiana, surrendered to troops under General Nathaniel P. Banks on July 9, the entire stretch of the Mississippi was again under Union control.

Grant, who undertook many risks and emerged victorious, brilliantly executed the Vicksburg campaign. As a result, he was promoted to the command of all Union troops west of the Appalachians, the first step in his rise to general-in-chief by March 1864.

> "When you got below, and took Port Gibson, Grand Gulf, and vicinity, I thought you should go down the river and join Gen. Banks; and when you turned Northward East of the Big Black, I feared it was a mistake. I now wish to make the personal acknowledgment that you were right, and I was wrong."
>
> —Abraham Lincoln, congratulating Union General Ulysses S. Grant on the victory at Vicksburg

This Kurz & Allison painting depicts Confederate troops raising the flag of truce on July 4, 1863, after the siege of Vicksburg.

GETTYSBURG

A NEW BIRTH OF FREEDOM

Following the Battle of Chancellorsville in May 1863, General Robert E. Lee reorganized his army into three corps, led by lieutenant generals James Longstreet, Richard S. Ewell, and Ambrose P. Hill. Strengthened by new brigades, his Army of Northern Virginia fielded about 75,000 men, the strongest it had been in over a year.

Union general Joseph Hooker's Army of the Potomac remained a threat. Although defeated in the recent battle, Hooker's army maintained high morale and

General George G. Meade

troops that were anxious to engage in combat again. But the army began to shrink as nine-month and two-year regiments mustered out, taking about 20,000 soldiers from the ranks.

Lee had planned to march into Maryland again, but Hooker's movement preempted his plans. The Confederate general sought to draw the armies away from war-ravaged northern Virginia, gather supplies north of the Mason-Dixon Line, and perhaps win a victory on Northern soil. Since Europeans withheld recognition at this stage of the Civil War,

GETTYSBURG NATIONAL MILITARY PARK ★ GETTYSBURG, PENNSYLVANIA

The 40th New York infantry "Mozarters" are memorialized at Gettysburg. The unit fought in the battle and took part in Meade's cautious pursuit of Lee afterward. They were called "Mozarters" after the political faction in New York—Mozart, a rival group to Tammany Hall—which funded the outfitting, training, and transportation of the men.

BATTLEFIELD MONUMENTS

At present, there are 1,328 monuments, markers, and tablets on the Gettysburg battlefield. The first monument, in the shape of a memorial urn, was placed in the National Cemetery by survivors of the 1st Minnesota regiment in 1869. A decade later, the 2nd Massachusetts erected the first monument on the battlefield proper when the survivors placed it to mark the regiment's position on July 3 near Spangler's Spring. Most memorials were erected during the 1880s and 1890s. The latest additions, a monument and a position marker, were erected by descendants of the 11th Mississippi and were placed on the field in 2000. In 2002, a bronze sculpture by Ron Tunison was unveiled in the town's Evergreen Cemetery, honoring women of Gettysburg. It depicts Elizabeth Thorn, the cemetery caretaker's wife, mopping her brow, a shovel in her hand. Her husband was in the Union army. Thorn, six months pregnant, aided by her aged father, buried 91 bodies in the town cemetery.

North Carolina State Monument

John B. Bachelder created this isometric view of Gettysburg in the fall of 1863.

Lee reasoned that a Southern victory might convince the Lincoln administration to sue for peace.

The campaign in Gettysburg began in early June, as Lee began to shift troops away from Fredericksburg toward the Shenandoah Valley. Hooker sent his cavalry across the Rappahannock on June 9, engaging Jeb Stuart's Southern horsemen in a day-long battle at Brandy Station.

THE COLORFUL LIFE OF DAN SICKLES

Daniel E. Sickles (1819–1914) was a Democratic politician who was given a general's commission by the Lincoln administration to help bolster support for the war effort. Sickles was already well-known when the war began. As secretary to the American delegation in London, he took a New York prostitute with him and actually presented her to Queen Victoria. In 1859, Sickles shot and killed Philip Barton Key (Francis Scott Key's son), who had been having an affair with his wife. In the ensuing trial, his lawyers pleaded temporary insanity for the first time in American legal history and their client was acquitted. Sickles was wounded at Gettysburg, losing his right leg to a cannonball. He later gave the amputated limb to the Army Medical Museum, where it now reposes.

After the war, Sickles was American minister to Spain and helped establish a short-lived Spanish republic, but rumors of an affair with Queen Isabella II compromised his effectiveness. In later years, Sickles was again serving in Congress and authored the bill that established the Gettysburg National Military Park. But as chairman of the New York Gettysburg Battlefield Commission, he was accused of embezzlement and removed. Sickles's efforts to smear General Meade's name and accomplishments at Gettysburg have typified Sickles's extremely controversial life.

Ewell's corps struck the Federal garrison at Winchester, shattering the Yankees and sending survivors running. Ewell's three divisions continued across the Potomac and into southern Pennsylvania.

Meanwhile, Hooker's army headed north as cavalry from the opposing sides fought at Aldie, Middleburg, and Upperville.

As the rest of Lee's army moved across the Potomac, Hooker followed

A scene from the Gettysburg cyclorama, showing Union troops advancing

more slowly, unsure of Lee's intentions. The general had orders to protect Washington, but Hooker also wanted to use the Harper's Ferry garrison and part of his army to sever Lee's supply line with Virginia. When the War Department refused Hooker's request, he sent in his resignation. Lincoln accepted Hooker's tender and replaced him with Major General George G. Meade on June 28, as the army gathered near Frederick, Maryland.

Lee's army, by late June, was mostly in the vicinity of Chambersburg, Pennsylvania, while Ewell's corps was scattered, a division at York and two divisions approaching the western defenses of Harrisburg, which was defended by state militia called into service in response to Lee's invasion. Troops from New York also flocked into the area to oppose a Confederate advance. But very quickly one of Longstreet's spies managed bring word that the enemy was across the Potomac and heading north under a new general. Lee recalled Ewell's units and began to concentrate his army just to the east of Chambersburg.

Upon taking command, Meade brought his army closer together and contemplated fighting a defensive battle behind the line of Pipe Creek, Maryland. But he gave his subordinates discretionary orders as well. On June 30, Union cavalry led by John Buford entered the crossroads town of Gettysburg and sighted enemy troops to the west on the Chambersburg Pike. The next morning, July 1, Confederate troops from Hill's corps appeared on the road to Gettysburg and engaged Buford's cavalry, fighting dismounted. Buford's outnumbered troopers held off the first Confederate attacks until infantry from Major General John F. Reynolds's First Corps arrived on the scene and counterattacked, shattering two Confederate brigades and capturing one of their commanders. Reynolds was killed early in the action and was replaced by his senior division commander, Abner Doubleday. The Union Eleventh Corps arrived and extended the First Corps line north of Gettysburg.

After a lull in the fighting, more Confederates arrived, another division

General James Longstreet

of Hill's corps and two of Ewell's, all returning from their abortive march on Harrisburg. Ewell's troops struck the Eleventh Corps line, outflanked it, and routed some of its units, pursuing the fugitives through the streets of Gettysburg. Meanwhile, the outnumbered First Corps inflicted and received heavy casualties as Hill's divisions pushed it, too, back through Gettysburg. The survivors were beginning to regroup on Cemetery Hill south of the town when Winfield Scott Hancock, Meade's Second Corps commander, arrived on the field, sent there by Meade to assess the situation. Hancock helped get the troops in order as units from two more Federal corps arrived. He recommended fighting at Gettysburg, a decision Meade had already made, having sent orders to the rest of the army to march there.

Throughout the night, units of the two armies converged on Gettysburg. By early morning of July 2, Meade had fashioned a J-shaped line of battle, stretching from Culp's Hill on the right to

SERGEANT AMOS HUMISTON

Amos Humiston was a member of Company C, 154th New York, a regiment that served in the ill-fated Eleventh Corps at Gettysburg. Humiston's regiment and the rest of its brigade rushed into the town to cover the retreat of the broken corps on the afternoon of July 1. The brigade was drawn up in battle line when it was overwhelmed by attacking Confederates. Sergeant Humiston's body was found in Stratton Street after Union soldiers reoccupied the town. Clutched in his hand was a photograph of his three children, the last thing the sergeant saw before he died. But no personal information was found on Humiston's body. Who were the children? The body was buried and the photograph was copied and circulated widely throughout the North. Finally, Humiston's widow, living in Cattaraugus County, New York, saw the photo and identified the children as her own. Proceeds from the sale of this now-famous photo were used to found the Soldiers Orphans Home at Gettysburg. The widow Humiston was its first matron.

The Humiston children

Did You Know?

Just three days before the Battle of Gettysburg, George Gordon Meade was appointed by President Lincoln to command the Union army, a position he assumed with some reluctance. Nicknamed "The Old Snapping Turtle," Meade wrote to his wife, "You know how reluctant we have both been to see me placed in this position. [But] I had nothing to do but to accept and exert my utmost abilities to command success." While Meade led the Union to a much-needed victory at Gettysburg, it was a success that came at great cost: Gettysburg became the bloodiest battle in American history, with approximately 51,000 combined casualties.

Lee's retreat as sketched by Albert Bobbett in 1905

nearby Cemetery Hill to the west, then southward along Cemetery Ridge to Little Round Top, a jagged hill partially cleared of timber by local farmers. Meade planned to wait until his entire army was on the field before attacking—his biggest corps, John Sedgwick's Sixth, was more than 30 miles away and would not reach the field until later that day.

Lee, forced into an unwanted battle by his subordinates, nevertheless concentrated his army and decided to attack the enemy against the wishes of Longstreet, his most trusted corps commander. Lee felt he could not afford to wait for Meade's attack because of a lack of supplies and his fear that enemy militia might move upon his rear flank. Besides, Lee thought his veteran soldiers could whip the Yankees in a fair fight. Lee ordered Longstreet to take his two divisions (George Pickett's was still en route) and attack up the Emmitsburg Road toward Cemetery Hill. Faulty reconnaissance led Lee to believe that Meade's line did not extend all the way south along Cemetery Ridge. Thus, Longstreet would assail Meade's left while Ewell attacked Culp's Hill to pin the enemy in place. Hill's corps, in the center, would assist the other two corps and attack if the opportunity presented itself.

General James E. B. Stuart

Subsequent maneuvers on both sides remain enshrouded in controversy. Longstreet waited for direct orders and did not begin his march until 11:00 a.m. By the time his lead brigade arrived in the vicinity of the Emmitsburg Road (after taking a circuitous route to avoid being seen by Federal signal corpsmen on Little Round Top), Longstreet found that the enemy had moved forward to occupy high ground along that road. Union major general Daniel E. Sickles, a politically minded general with no prior military training, was in charge of Meade's Third

Corps. Sickles was assigned to that part of the line south of Hancock on Cemetery Ridge, but he did not like his position and after much wrangling with Meade and other officers, took it upon himself to move forward to seize high ground along the Emmitsburg Road, thereby ignoring Little Round Top and placing his command forward of the main Union line. His corps were arrayed in a V-shaped salient.

Meade did not learn of Sickles's mid-afternoon move until later, when he

THE GETTYSBURG GUN

During the terrific artillery duel preceding Pickett's Charge on the afternoon of July 3, an exploding ball from a Confederate cannon struck the muzzle of one of the 12-pounder Napoleon cannons in Battery B, 1st Rhode Island, killing two of its crewmen. The survivors removed their comrades and prepared to fire another round. But as they loaded their own solid shot into the muzzle, it became stuck because the enemy round had dented the barrel. The cannon was retired and retained as a trophy, and is on display today in the Rhode Island State House. Only a few years ago, the cannon was subjected to an X-ray scan. It was discovered that the barrel contained two powder charges that dated back to that fateful July day in 1863.

The Gettysburg Gun on display in the Rhode Island State House

> **"Thousands of our brave boys are left upon the enemy's soil and in my opinion our army will never be made of such material again."**
>
> —*Confederate Private Alexander McNeill*

convened a meeting of his corps commanders and discovered that Sickles had moved forward. Sickles offered to return to the main line, but at 3:30 p.m., Longstreet's artillery opened fire. Meade told Sickles to remain in line and went back to bring up reinforcements. By the time the fighting died down after nightfall, Meade had sent in five brigades from Hancock's Second Corps, the entire Fifth Corps, some of the depleted First Corps, a division from the Twelfth Corps, and brigades from the tired Sixth Corps as they arrived on the field. Longstreet's eight brigades, assisted by one of Hill's divisions, fought all these Union troops. Union troops reached Little Round Top just minutes before Confederate troops attacked, saving the Union left flank. Combat swirled back and forth across a 19-acre wheatfield (later called "The Wheatfield"), among the boulders of Devil's Den, and in farmer Sherfy's Peach Orchard. Sickles himself was hit in the leg by a cannonball; his shattered limb was later amputated. By day's end, the Union line had stabilized on Cemetery Ridge.

On the Union right, Edward Johnson's division charged forward to occupy abandoned Union breastworks of the Twelfth Corps on Culp's Hill, but a lone New York brigade held the crest of the hill. Reinforcements and darkness neutralized

The rock pile called the Devil's Den, where hidden Confederate snipers harassed Union troops on Little Round Top

further Confederate gains. Other Southern regiments charged the Union batteries on Cemetery Hill, but were repelled after a vicious hand-to-hand fight. That night, Meade and his corps commanders decided to stay and fight one more day. Lee, believing that Meade had weakened his center to stabilize his flanks, ordered Longstreet to assail the Federal center.

Gathering at Gettysburg on the first anniversary of battle

Fighting on July 3 erupted at daybreak when Union troops attacked the Confederates on Culp's Hill. By late morning, the firing had died down as the Confederates withdrew, their attacks having been repulsed by the Yankees. Meanwhile Confederate artillerist Edward Porter Alexander assembled a line of 120 cannons to bombard the Union center. The Rebel guns opened fire shortly after one o'clock; more than 80 Union cannons replied. The thunderous bombardment shook the ground and reportedly could be heard as far away as Pittsburgh and Philadelphia. The resulting thick smoke obscured targets and misled Southern cannoneers, who generally overshot Cemetery Ridge, thus causing havoc behind the Union lines.

As the bombardment died out, Longstreet sent George Pickett's three Virginia brigades forward, supported by troops from two of Hill's divisions. These units, estimated at between 10,500 and 15,000 men, marched bravely across the mile-wide valley between Seminary and Cemetery ridges, being blasted the entire way by Union artillery. As the survivors crossed the Emmitsburg Road, Union musketry took its toll. By the time the advance elements reached the

AN ASSASSIN AT GETTYSBURG

Nineteen-year-old Lewis Powell (alias Lewis Paine) marched into battle on July 2 with the 3nd Florida infantry, part of Colonel David Lang's brigade of Richard Anderson's division. Lang's three regiments encountered a Union artillery battery supported by the 19th Maine regiment. Before the Yankees fell back to Cemetery Ridge, they inflicted numerous casualties on the Floridians. Private Powell was hit in the right wrist by a rifle ball and was captured when Lee's army retreated. Powell eventually was moved into a Baltimore hospital. After recovering sufficiently, he worked as a hospital assistant and befriended a nurse, who possibly helped him escape from watching guards. On April 14, 1865, as John Wilkes Booth assassinated President Lincoln, Powell barged into the home of Secretary of State William H. Seward and attacked him. The wounded Seward survived, but Powell was caught and hanged along with three others convicted in the assassination plot.

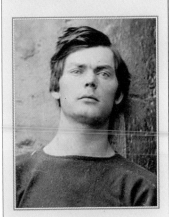
Lewis Powell

THE MASCOT OF THE 1st MARYLAND

Union general Thomas L. Kane recorded the following incident as Rebels charged his brigade on Culp's Hill during the fierce fighting on the morning of July 3: "A pet dog belonging to a company of the 1st Maryland (Confederate) charged with the regiment, ran ahead of them when their progress was arrested, and came in among the boys in blue, as if the dog supposed they were what in better days they might have been— merely men of another noisy hose or engine company, competing for precedence with his masters in the smoke of a burning building. At first, some of my men said, he barked in valorous glee; but I myself first saw him on three legs going between our own and the men in gray on the ground as though looking for a dead master, or seeking on which side he might find an explanation of the tragedy he had witnessed, intelligible to his canine apprehension. Regarding him as the only Christian-minded being on either side, I ordered him to be honorably buried."

Union line, Pickett's Charge had been disrupted. Union counterattacks flanked both ends of the Southern line, and the attack collapsed after briefly penetrating the Union line near a copse of trees. Half the attackers had been killed, wounded, or captured.

Pickett's Charge became the decisive repulsion of Lee's army. East of Gettysburg, Jeb Stuart's horsemen moved to attack the Union rear but were countered by Yankee mounted troops led by David Gregg and George A. Custer. After a spirited battle, Stuart withdrew. A belated Union cavalry attack on the Confederate right failed, bringing to an end the three days of Gettysburg.

Meade's army of approximately 85,000 men suffered a loss of 22,807 (3,149 killed, 14,501 wounded, 5,157

captured or missing). Lee, with a battlefield strength of around 75,000, lost at least 28,000 soldiers. His army remained in position on July 4, but that night, in the midst of a hard rain, it began a retreat to Virginia. Meade, his army badly battered, followed but was unable to bring Lee to battle. Rain swelled the Potomac River and Union cavalry cut Lee's pontoon bridge, but the Confederates dug in and gave Meade's army cause for caution. By the time Meade was ready to attack, Lee had slipped across the Potomac. By the end of July, both armies were back in northern Virginia. The Gettysburg Campaign, though a bitter defeat for Lee, did not end the war.

Northerners quickly realized the significance of the battle and began to plan for a park to preserve the battlefield. Union dead were gathered together in a new cemetery adjacent to the civilian Evergreen Cemetery on Cemetery Hill. Formal dedication ceremonies were planned for the afternoon of November 19. The featured speaker was noted orator

The Battle of Culp's Hill at Gettysburg

Edward Everett. Almost as an afterthought, somebody thought to invite President Lincoln, who accepted the invitation to say a few words.

After listening to Everett for two hours, Lincoln arose to deliver his own speech. The president's now-famous Gettysburg Address contained just 272 words and lasted about two minutes. Its brevity meant photographers were unable to capture Lincoln's speech, but Everett quickly realized that the president, in his own folksy style, had articulated to his nation the higher ideals for which the war was being waged. Everett recognized that history would remember that speech longer than his own. "All men are created equal," said the president. This civil war was being fought to preserve the nation and its experiment in republican government. The war would produce a "new

birth of freedom." Thus, "government of the people, by the people, for the people, shall not perish from the earth."

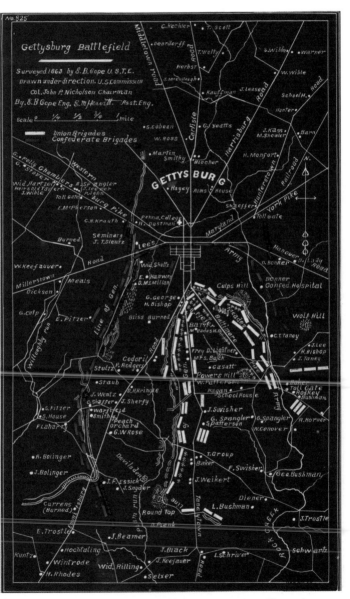

Map of the Gettysburg battlefield showing troops, artillery points, roads, railroads, and dwellings

"We cannot dedicate—we can not consecrate—we can not hallow—this ground. The brave men, living and dead, who struggled here, have consecrated it, far above our poor power to add or detract."

—Abraham Lincoln, *Gettysburg Address, November 19, 1863*

The Battle of Gettysburg by John Sartain vividly shows the clash between Union and Confederate troops during Pickett's Charge, the fateful third day of the battle.

This Kurz & Allison print of the Battle of Chickamauga depicts the fierce confrontation as Confederate troops break through the Union lines on September 20, 1863.

CHICKAMAUGA

CONFEDERATE HIGH TIDE

VISITOR INFORMATION

Name Chickamauga & Chattanooga

Classification National Military Park

Established August 19, 1890. Transferred from War Department August 10, 1933. Boundary changes: August 9, 1939; March 5, 1942; June 24, 1948

Contact P.O. Box 2128, Fort Oglethorpe, GA 30742

Phone 706-866-9241

Website www.nps.gov/chch

Acreage 8,119.11 (Federal: 8,102.32; Nonfederal: 16.79)

Points of Focus Brotherton Cabin, Chattanooga National Cemetery, Cravens House, Lookout Mountain, Missionary Ridge, Orchard Knob, Snodgrass Hill, Sunset Rock, Wilder Brigade Monument

Tours/Paths 7-mile self-guided driving tour, various hiking and horse trails

Hours Chickamauga Battlefield Visitor Center open daily from 8:30 a.m. to 5:00 p.m. Lookout Mountain Battlefield Visitor Center open daily from 9:00 a.m. to 5:00 p.m. (6:00 p.m. in the summer)

Park Fee Free ($3 admission charge for Point Park)

Programs Living History programs, 26-minute orientation film, Junior Ranger program

Facilities Point Park, two visitor centers

Following the Battle of Stones River, Major General William S. Rosecrans's Union Army of the Cumberland went into winter quarters at Murfreesboro and rebuilt its strength. General Braxton Bragg's Army of Tennessee retreated from the area and went into position in the interior of Tennessee, some 40 miles from Murfreesboro. Here the armies stayed even as President Lincoln badgered Rosecrans to resume the offensive to ensure that Rebel reinforcements did not advance to Vicksburg or join Lee's Virginia army.

General Braxton Bragg

Rosecrans finally began to move in June 1863. In a series of brilliant maneuvers known as the Tullahoma Campaign, the Yankee general pushed Bragg's army out of central Tennessee with a minimum of fighting. Bragg retreated to Chattanooga and prepared to face Rosecrans. But Rosecrans failed to pursue Bragg and instead sent his three corps through the mountains west and southwest of the city, threatening Bragg's supplies. Bragg hurriedly evacuated Chattanooga and withdrew into northern Georgia.

Rosecrans's mobile field army of some 58,000 men began to withdraw slightly

CHICKAMAUGA & CHATTANOOGA NATIONAL MILITARY PARK ★ FORT OGLETHORPE, GEORGIA

A MEDAL OF HONOR

First Lieutenant Arthur MacArthur of the 24th Wisconsin was only 18 years old when his regiment charged up the steep slopes of Missionary Ridge. When the color bearer fell down exhausted, MacArthur grabbed the silk banner and led his men forward, shouting "On, Wisconsin!" as Confederate cannons blasted the attackers with canister. MacArthur planted the regimental flag on the enemy breastworks as his regiment swept over the crest of the ridge. In 1890, he received a Medal of Honor for his heroic deeds that day. MacArthur was later promoted to colonel of the regiment. His son, Douglas, was the famous army commander in the Pacific during World War II and in Korea.

First Lieutenant Arthur MacArthur Jr.

Umbrella Rock on Lookout Mountain

once the general realized that his three corps were spaced too far apart to support one another. Bragg was being reinforced from Mississippi, Alabama, and Virginia; General Lee dispatched General James Longstreet and two divisions by rail to help him. When these troops arrived, Bragg's army actually outnumbered the Federals, a rarity in Civil War battles.

THE BATTLE OF CHICKAMAUGA

Rosecrans collected his troops on the west side of Chickamauga Creek, some 20 miles south of Chattanooga. Bragg planned to cross the creek north of Rosecrans's left flank and sever Union communications with Chattanooga. This would force Rosecrans to retreat westward through the mountains, thus allowing Bragg's troops to isolate and destroy the Yankees.

But Bragg's plan went awry from the beginning, and the anticipated battle did not materialize until September 19. On that day, Bragg's right wing under command of Lieutenant General Leonidas Polk crossed the creek and assailed the Federal left flank, the first attack in a series of charges and countercharges that took place all along the 4-mile lines of battle. Rosecrans had stationed Major General George H. Thomas and his Fourteenth Corps on the Union left. Thomas, one of the Union's all-around best corps commanders, deployed his men in the densely wooded terrain and repelled all of Polk's attacks. Farther south more Southern troops went into action, but by the end of the day all attacks had been repulsed. But Longstreet's troops began to arrive that night, giving Bragg the resolve to renew combat.

Fighting resumed on September 20, as Polk's troops hurled themselves against Thomas's line once more. Thomas began to call upon Rosecrans for reinforcements for his hard-pressed men. One of Rosecrans's staff officers then mistakenly told the general that there was a gap in the Union line farther south; in fact the officer had simply missed seeing the line, which had been hidden by dense trees. Rosecrans then ordered General Thomas J. Wood to take his division out of line and fill in the gap. Wood was dumbfounded—there were troops on his left. But the order was imperative, and he had earlier been castigated for not obeying orders with alacrity. Rather than argue with his superior, Wood complied.

Major General George H. Thomas

As Wood's troops vacated the line and moved north, Longstreet's troops rolled forward and struck the gap Wood had created. The Southern attack overwhelmed the Union right flank, which cracked under the pressure, and regiments retreated from the field toward Chattanooga, including Rosecrans and two of his corps commanders. Jubilant Confederates captured dozens of cannons as the army in blue melted away.

But Thomas's corps continued to hold its ground, strengthened by individual units that rallied and extended his line to cover the vital Snodgrass Hill. General Gordon Granger, acting without orders, brought fresh reserve brigades onto the field and went into position with Thomas. The entire Confederate army then assailed Thomas, but the Union line held until dark, when Thomas retired to Chattanooga. The general fairly earned his sobriquet "The Rock of Chickamauga."

Union casualties totaled 16,179, but Bragg's victorious army suffered a loss of 17,804 soldiers. Bragg followed Rosecrans to Chattanooga, a city he put under siege by occupying the high ground of Missionary Ridge and Lookout Mountain, which dominated the city and restricted access to the besieged defenders.

CHICKAMAUGA: THE RIVER OF DEATH

Cherokee Indians named this northern Georgia creek the "River of Death" because of the many intertribal battles along the stream. The bloodbath there in September 1863 only added to its meaning. And like many other scenes of combat, Chickamauga has its share of haunted tales. Veterans of the 125th Ohio erected a monument surmounted by a carved tiger, in honor of the regiment's nickname, "Opdycke's Tigers." Witnesses maintain that they have seen an otherwordly tiger prowling the battlefield at night, supposedly searching for its emerald eyes; others have been frightened by eerie green eyes staring at them through the darkness. Modern-day reenactors have encountered ghostly men from both armies, still fighting the battle over a century later.

Death at Chickamauga did not end with the Civil War. When war with Spain erupted in 1898, the government established a training camp on the battlefield. Named Camp Thomas, it was the assembly point for two army corps and associated troops, about 60,000 men in all. Lack of rail transportation meant that supplies were frequently delayed, and the troops suffered accordingly. Improper sites for camps, lack of strict discipline over the use of latrines, and close confinement of thousands of men led to a wave of typhoid fever, killing 425 men, hospitalizing thousands, and leading to a government inquiry into the problems at Camp Thomas.

Rosecrans was relieved of command and replaced by Thomas. General Grant, having been placed in command of all Union forces west of the Appalachians following his victory at Vicksburg, arrived on the scene in person to direct operations.

Behind Grant came General William T. Sherman with more than 15,000 troops from Grant's army in Mississippi. From Virginia, Major General Joseph Hooker was placed in command of units from two corps from Meade's army that were sent by rail from northern Virginia to Bridgeport, Alabama, whence they marched overland toward Chattanooga. Once all these troops arrived, Bragg would be outnumbered, because he had detached Longstreet and sent him

Louis Prang lithograph of the assault on Missionary Ridge

toward Knoxville, which had been occupied by Union troops under General Ambrose E. Burnside.

THE BATTLE OF CHATTANOOGA

By late October, Union troops sallied from Chattanooga to Brown's Ferry across the Tennessee, thus opening the "Cracker Line," a new supply route into the city. Grant then planned an elaborate series of attacks to drive Bragg's troops from Chattanooga. The Battle of Chattanooga began on November 23, when units from Thomas's army left their defenses and captured Orchard Knob, giving Thomas room to maneuver.

On the 24th, troops from Hooker's command began to drive the enemy from Lookout Mountain, its peak 1,100 feet above the valley floor. Fog enshrouded much of the battle from onlookers, so that it was called "the battle above the clouds." Hooker's more numerous troops surged forward and drove the enemy from the mountain, threatening Bragg's left flank.

The major battle took place on November 25. Hooker, assigned to attack Bragg's left, was stymied by Chattanooga

Confederate prisoners waiting for the train in Chattanooga

Creek. On the Union left, Sherman's troops assailed Bragg's right at Tunnel Hill, but the stubborn defenders under Patrick Cleburne's command repelled all of Sherman's attacks and even counterattacked, capturing some prisoners. To relieve pressure on Sherman, Grant ordered Thomas to send four divisions forward to seize Confederate rifle pits at the base of Missionary Ridge. Once this was accomplished, however, Thomas's troops failed to heed orders to stop. Southern troops on the military crest of the ridge high above them continued to fire. Lacking orders, units began to head uphill until it appeared to Grant and Thomas, watching in horror, that the entire line was advancing. But instead of a bloody repulse, Thomas's troops surged forward and Bragg's army began to retreat in disorder.

By the end of the day, Bragg was in full retreat and Chattanooga was a major Federal victory. Losses totaled 5,815 Union soldiers and more than 6,700 Rebels, but Bragg had lost 40 cannons and his army was badly demoralized. That winter, President Davis replaced Bragg with General Joseph E. Johnston in an effort to restore the army's shaken morale.

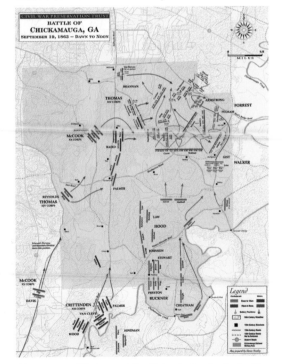
Movement of Union and Confederate troops during the Battle of Chickamauga

"The *elan* of the Southern soldier was never seen after Chickamauga. . . . He fought stoutly to the last, but after Chickamauga, with the sullenness of despair and without the enthusiasm of hope. That 'barren victory' sealed the fate of the Confederacy."

—Confederate Lieutenant General D. H. Hill

VISITOR INFORMATION

Name Kennesaw Mountain

Classification National Battlefield Park

Established February 8, 1917. Transferred from War Department August 10, 1933; redesignated June 26, 1935. Boundary change: August 9, 1939

Contact 900 Kennesaw Mountain Drive, Kennesaw, GA 30152

Phone 770-427-4686 x 0

Website www.nps.gov/kemo

Acreage 2,884.14 (Federal: 2,879.60; Nonfederal: 4.54)

Points of Focus Cheatham Hill, Kennesaw Mountain Overlook, Kolb's Farm, Pigeon Hill

Tours/Paths Self-guided driving tour of the battlefield; 2-mile, 5-mile, 10-mile, and 16-mile walking/horse/ hiking trails

Hours Visitor center open daily from 8:30 a.m. to 5:00 p.m. All facilities closed Thanksgiving Day, December 25, and January 1

Park Fee Free

Programs 18-minute orientation film, Living History programs (summer season only), Junior Ranger program

Facilities Visitor center, three activity areas, two picnic areas, museum

KENNESAW
ON THE ROAD TO ATLANTA

The Kennesaw Mountain battlefield in Georgia is the lone park memorial to men in blue and gray who contended with each other over the fate of Atlanta in 1864. This pivotal campaign began in May 1864 and ended with the Union capture of Atlanta on September 2. Major General William T. Sherman's success in this campaign helped ensure that Abraham Lincoln would win the presidential election of 1864, and by doing so, it ensured that the Union would pursue final victory in the Civil War.

General Joseph E. Johnston

Part of the overall Union strategy for 1864 involved General Sherman's "army group," based in the Chattanooga area. Sherman, in charge of all departments from the Mississippi to the Appalachians, had three armies under his command; together, they added up to more than 110,000 soldiers. Largest was Major General George H. Thomas's Army of the Cumberland, composed of three infantry and one cavalry corps. Also present was much of the Army of the Tennessee, now led by Major General James B. McPherson, who had two corps on hand and another

General Sherman watches the Battle of Kennesaw Mountain as his frontal assault on the entrenched positions of the Confederates is repulsed with heavy losses in what became a costly Union defeat.

> **"The sun beaming down on our uncovered heads, the thermometer being one hundred and ten degrees in the shade, and a solid line of blazing fire right from the muzzles of the Yankee guns being poured right into our very faces . . . ."**
>
> —*Private Samuel R. Watkins, 1st Tennessee CSA*

> **"Our lines are now in close contact and the fighting incessant, with a good deal of artillery. As fast as we gain one position, the enemy has another all ready, but I think he will soon have to let go Kennesaw, which is the key to the whole country."**
>
> —*Union General William Tecumseh Sherman*

en route. Finally, Major General John M. Schofield assembled 13,000 men of the Army of the Ohio, essentially a reinforced infantry corps.

Opposed to Sherman was General Joseph E. Johnston and his 40,000-man Army of Tennessee. Johnston had two infantry corps available for duty, with an additional 9,000 men present in Joseph Wheeler's cavalry corps. Once the fighting began, Johnston would receive an additional corps of reinforcements. Throughout the campaign that followed, Johnston was tasked with preventing Sherman from penetrating deep into Southern territory, and also with covering Atlanta.

Sherman began the campaign by maneuvering Johnston out of his strong natural position at Dalton and Rocky Face Ridge. Johnston's smaller army had to fall back when its supply line was threatened, but delay by General McPherson robbed Sherman of the opportunity to completely isolate Johnston's army. The result was a two-day battle at the railroad town of Resaca, Georgia, on May 14–15; the two armies suffered a combined loss of 7,000 men.

Entrenchments at Kennesaw Mountain, Georgia

Kurz & Allison lithograph depicting the Battle of Kennesaw Mountain

COLONEL DAN McCOOK

One of the Federal brigades assaulting Kennesaw was led by Colonel Daniel McCook, a member of Ohio's "Fighting McCooks." Two McCook families sent 17 men into the Union army; their ranks ranged from private to chaplain to general.

Daniel McCook was born in 1834 and was a former law partner of William T. Sherman. McCook served in a Kansas regiment at Wilson's Creek and was later promoted to colonel of the 52nd Ohio. Sherman himself personally selected his old law partner's brigade to lead the assault on Kennesaw. Knowing the rough odds against success, Colonel McCook gave his men a pep talk by reciting the verses of "Horatius' Speech," a popular poem by British poet Thomas Macaulay.

The sad story of McCook's assault was one repeated all too often during the war. Attacking the Confederate strong point known as the Dead Angle in a desperate uphill battle, the Ohioans suffered heavy losses—more than 135 casualties, about 35 percent of the unit's strength. The Yankees reached the Rebel works and engaged in bloody hand-to-hand combat. "Colonel Dan" mounted the enemy breastwork and called for the colors to be forwarded. He was shot in the chest and collapsed. McCook died on July 17, having been promoted to brigadier general the previous day.

Johnston was again forced to retreat when elements of the Union army moved south, threatening Johnston's rear lines.

During his retreat, Johnston divided his army, hoping to prod Sherman into doing the same. Then, the Confederates would quickly reunite on familiar ground and defeat a portion of Sherman's larger army. But as Johnston prepared to strike, he received erroneous reports of more Union troops and instead was forced to fall back slightly and regroup. Sherman, largely following the course of the Western & Atlantic Railroad, which he used for supplies, then decided

General John B. Hood

HUMANITY IN THE MIDST OF BATTLE

During the desperate Federal assault on June 27, gunfire ignited dry brush on the mountainside, starting several brushfires that threatened the wounded Union soldiers lying helpless near the flames. About half an hour after one charge, recalled Captain Robert D. Smith of the 2nd Tennessee, Confederates stopped firing and called to their enemy to come and rescue their wounded comrades. The firing stopped as the Rebels watched their enemies gather up the wounded and return to their lines. Such scenes happened on many a battlefield during the war, when nature threatened man's inhumanity to man. The bloodletting stopped long enough for the boys in blue and gray to save their comrades from burning to death.

Wounded being removed from the battle in a sketch of combat action

to swing to the west to get around Johnston's left.

But Johnston blocked Sherman yet again. The result was a series of engagements from May 25 to June 4, known as Dallas, New Hope Church, and Pickett's Mill. Skirmishers of both armies aptly named one site the "Hell Hole." Neither side gained an advantage; Sherman then decided to move east toward the railroad again.

When Sherman began moving east, Johnston fell back to a range of mountains that protected his supply base at Marietta. Ten days of rain hampered military movements, but on June 10, Sherman again moved forward. Johnston fell back yet again to an even stronger and more compact position on Kennesaw Mountain. Four more days of rain slowed Sherman's pursuit as his army moved into position opposite the Rebels.

Sherman sent Joseph Hooker's Twentieth Corps from Thomas's army to the Union right to outflank the Kennesaw position, but in the June 22 Battle of Kolb's Farm, Confederates from John B. Hood's corps blunted the Union attack. Then, Schofield's men went into

position on Hooker's right, but found more Rebels to their front. Reports of these defenses prompted Sherman to try a frontal assault on the steep mountain. Sherman believed that Johnston might have weakened his seemingly impregnable position in order to confront the Union left, and a direct attack of his own might succeed.

Sherman readied two assault columns from Thomas's and McPherson's commands, keeping ample reserves on hand to exploit any breakthrough. But the Battle of Kennesaw Mountain on June 27 was a complete failure. Neither Union column made any headway. And even though elements of the attacking regiments actually reached the Confederate fortifications and engaged in hand-to-hand combat, the Rebel defenders of Patrick Cleburne's and Benjamin F. Cheatham's divisions held firm and repelled the desperate assaults. Even so, some of the attacking units dug in only yards in front of the Rebels; constant sniping over the next six days wore both sides down. Sherman's army lost more than 3,000 men while Johnston reported a loss of about 1,000.

Sherman then resorted to another

flanking maneuver and Johnston fell back across the Chattahoochie River, the last major barrier before Atlanta. But Johnston was unable to prevent Union troops from crossing, and after Johnston fell back to Atlanta's defenses, President Davis replaced him with Hood, a twice-wounded general known for his aggressiveness. Hood immediately sallied forth, but in a series of three battles around Atlanta—Peach Tree Creek (July 20), Atlanta (July 22), and Ezra Church (July 28)—his army suffered a total of 18,000 casualties.

After these three battles, Sherman erected siege earthworks and sent his cavalry to disrupt Southern supply lines. But when his cavalry failed miserably in these raids, Sherman moved south with most of his army, cutting off the railroad at Jonesboro, south of Atlanta. After two days of fighting at Jonesboro (August 31–September 1), Hood evacuated Atlanta, burning all supplies his men could not take with them. Sherman's army entered Atlanta on September 2 as Hood withdrew to Lovejoy's Station. After Hood moved north in an attempt to interdict Sherman's supply line, Sherman divided his army, sending Thomas to confront Hood's invasion of Tennessee while he took 60,000 men and marched across Georgia to the sea.

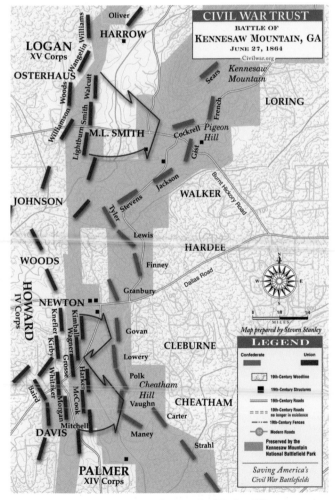

Movement of Union troops during the Battle of Kennesaw

Did You Know?

The name "Kennesaw" (pronounced "Gah-nee-sah") is a Cherokee word that means "cemetery" or "burial ground." Kennesaw became a literal burial ground in 1864, when it was fought as part of the Atlanta campaign. The campaign included 100,000 Union soldiers, 63,000 Confederate soldiers, and 35,000 Union horses. More than 67,000 men were killed or captured during the campaign.

It was at Fort Stevens that Early's men probed Washington's defenses. While Abraham Lincoln observed the situation in person, he came under hostile gunfire. Captain Oliver Wendell Holmes, Jr., a future Supreme Court justice, did not recognize the president and yelled at him to get down.

MONOCACY

THE BATTLE THAT SAVED WASHINGTON

VISITOR INFORMATION

Name Monocacy

Classification National Battlefield

Established October 21, 1976

Contact 5201 Urbana Pike, Frederick, MD 21704-7307

Phone 301-662-3515

Website www.nps.gov/mono

Acreage 1,647.01 (Federal: 1,310.24; Nonfederal: 336.77)

Points of Focus Gambrill Mill, Georgetown Pike, Monocacy Junction, Thomas Farm, Worthington Farm, Worthington-McKinney Ford

Tours/Paths Half-mile walking trail, 4-mile self-guided driving trail, Worthington Farm walking trail

Hours Visitor center open daily from 8:30 a.m. to 5:00 p.m. Closed Thanksgiving Day, December 25

Park Fee Free

Programs Self-guided driving tour, electronic orientation map, auto tour, interactive computer programs, Junior Ranger program

Facilities Visitor center, sheltered picnic area (open mid-April through October)

In June 1864, General David Hunter's Union army advanced to Lynchburg, Virginia, before retreating across the mountains into West Virginia, where General Lee had sent an entire corps of his army to confront the Yankees. Led by General Jubal A. Early, Southern troops then cleared the Shenandoah Valley of Union soldiers.

Early then chose to move his army across the Potomac into Maryland. As his army gathered supplies and ripped up the tracks of the Baltimore & Ohio Railroad, Early decided to head for Washington and threaten the city, seeking to draw off troops from Grant's army at Petersburg. To oppose the enemy advance, General Lew Wallace gathered about 3,000 men and deployed them along the east bank of the Monocacy River at Monocacy Junction, where the railroad tracks split toward Harper's Ferry and Frederick. On July 8, General James B. Ricketts's division of the Sixth Corps arrived from Petersburg, boosting Wallace's strength. The rest of the corps was still en route, detached by Grant in case they were needed.

Early's skirmishers probed the Union positions along the Monocacy

MONOCACY NATIONAL BATTLEFIELD ★ FREDERICK, MARYLAND

"Major, we haven't taken Washington, but we scared Abe Lincoln like hell!"

—*Confederate Lieutenant Jubal Early to Major Kyd Douglas*

on July 9. Southern horsemen located a ford beyond the Union left flank, and Early sent John B. Gordon's infantry division to secure the crossing as other units cautiously edged forward farther north. Wallace deployed Ricketts's men to face Gordon, but the more numerous Southerners lapped around his flanks and Ricketts had to withdraw. Wallace pulled back the rest of his units as Southern troops threatened to cross at two other bridges. The Yankees retreated toward Baltimore to protect that city

General John B. Gordon

from Confederate attack. Wallace had suffered more than 1,880 casualties; Early lost about 800 men.

But Wallace had delayed the Confederates by a day. When Early's men began to probe the Washington defenses on July 11, the rest of the Sixth Corps arrived to bolster the defenders. President Lincoln himself came under fire at Fort Stevens while he watched Union skirmishers in battle. Early became persuaded that he could not capture the city and thus withdrew.

An 1863 drawing of a railroad bridge at Monocacy

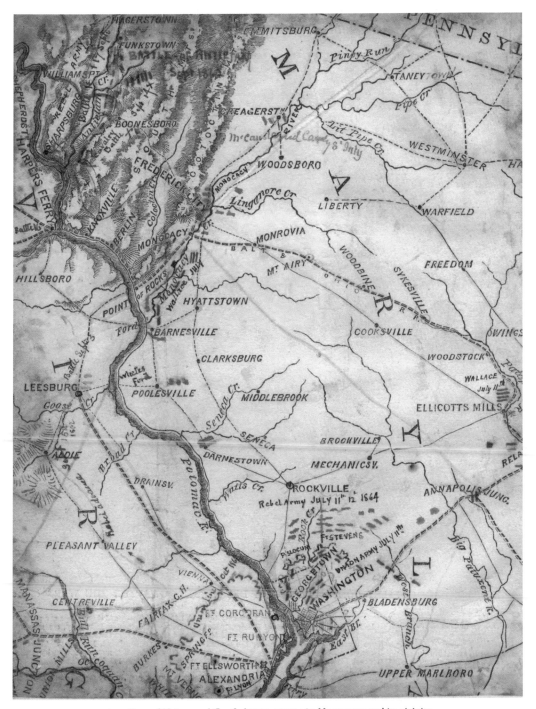

Location of Union and Confederate troops in Monocacy and its vicinity

Did You Know?

Union Major General Lew Wallace, who commanded the troops at Monocacy and prevented the capture of the nation's capital, became the Union army's youngest general when he was promoted in 1862. After the war, Wallace served on the military commission that tried the men accused of attempting to assassinate Abraham Lincoln. He went on to write *Ben Hur: A Tale of the Christ*, considered the most influential Christian book of the 19th century.

VISITOR INFORMATION

Name Petersburg

Classification National Battlefield

Established July 3, 1926

Contact 1539 Hickory Hill Road, Petersburg, VA 23803

Phone 804-732-3531

Website www.nps.gov/pete

Acreage Park—2,659.19 (Federal: 2,653.43; Nonfederal: 5.76). Cemetery—8.72 (all Federal)

Points of Focus City Point, Confederate Battery 5, Confederate Battery 8, Confederate Battery 9, the Crater, Five Forks, Fort Conahey, Fort Fisher, Fort Gregg, Fort Haskell, Fort Sedgwick, Fort Stedman, Fort Wadsworth, Poplar Grove National Cemetery, Taylor Farm

Tours/Paths 26 miles of self-guided driving tours, various walking trails

Hours Visitor center open daily from 9:00 a.m. to 5:00 p.m. Closed Thanksgiving Day, December 25, and January 1

Park Fee $3 per person or $5 per vehicle; $15 per individual annual pass

Programs Ranger-led talks, Junior Ranger program, Living History programs (summer season only), Petersburg National Battlefield VirtualCache Program

Facilities Two visitor centers, museum, bookstore

PETERSBURG
THE KEY TO RICHMOND

After suffering a repulse at Cold Harbor, General Grant decided to cross the James River and attack the railroad hub of Petersburg, 23 miles south of Richmond. Grant directed General Meade, in command of the Army of the Potomac, to send most of his troops across the James, leaving a single corps, General Warren's Fifth, to mask the change of position. In the meantime, Grant ordered General Benjamin F. Butler, whose Army of the James was entrenched at Bermuda Hundred, to also send troops to attack Petersburg. If the attacks could capture the city before Lee could reinforce its defenders, Grant was sure Lee would have to abandon Richmond.

But Grant's plan went awry almost from the beginning, even though Meade directed an effective withdrawal in front of Lee's army that completely took the great Southern leader by surprise. The hot June weather, exacerbated by a lack of rain, coupled with the severe loss of so many Union officers and men since the campaign had begun in May, stymied the Army

General Ulysses S. Grant

Federal soldiers removing artillery from a Confederate fortification at the battle of Petersburg, Virginia, April 1865

BOLTON'S BULLET

William J. Bolton (1833–1906) served in the 51st Pennsylvania from 1861–1865, first as a captain of Company A, then as a major, and finally as colonel. He was twice wounded: at Antietam, a bullet passed through his face; in the Crater at Petersburg, Bolton was hit yet again in the same spot, but the bullet lodged in his throat. Doctors were unable to locate and remove the object. Seventeen years later, in 1881, during a fit of coughing, the bullet was dislodged and plopped into the colonel's hand. He kept it as a souvenir of his wartime service.

Colonel William J. Bolton

of the Potomac. Troops from Butler's army began to attack the outer defenses of Petersburg on June 15, chasing back the city's comparatively few defenders. The assaulting troops included a division of black soldiers, who gleefully took prisoners and weapons at some of the enemy fortifications.

But a lack of effective orders spelled doom for the Yankees. Fearing a trap because the early attacks encountered so few defenders, Union commanders remained cautious; by the time more troops were present, Lee had guessed where Grant was heading and was shifting his army hurriedly into Petersburg's defenses. The Union attacks sputtered to a halt on June 18. Grant's men had

Federal supplies deposited on the landing at City Point, Virginia

suffered 11,000 casualties, and even though they occupied many Confederate earthworks, Rebels had already built even more formidable lines closer to the city.

So Grant decided to initiate siege operations. Union troops began digging trenches, laying out earthwork forts, and placing abatis in front of their works to discourage attacks from the Rebels. Union military engineers built a railroad right-of-way behind the lines to ensure a steady delivery of supplies from the base at City Point on the James River. From mid-June until April 1865, Union and Confederate soldiers remained locked in a deadly game of hide-and-seek as both sides erected formidable earthworks to deflect attacks from the other.

Grant's strategy during the siege was to keep lengthening the Union lines to make Lee match his moves, steadily weakening the enemy and forcing him to fight for control of the railroads that brought supplies from the South into Petersburg and Richmond. The first battle

The Fall of Petersburg, April 2, 1865

THEY SAID IT COULDN'T BE DONE

Once the siege lines stabilized at Petersburg in June 1864, Colonel Henry Pleasants of the 48th Pennsylvania received permission to dig a tunnel under a Confederate fort. General Meade and professional engineers at army headquarters scoffed at the idea, but corps commander Burnside approved. Starting 100 feet behind the Union front line on June 25, the 48th, which included more than 100 coal miners, began a tunnel that eventually reached 511 feet in length, then dug two lateral galleries, each about 40 feet in length, that would hold the powder to blow up the enemy fort. Working with improvised picks and having to scrounge for wood for tunnel supports, the troops completed the tunnel and its two laterals by July 23. Then, after packing 4 tons of gunpowder contained in sacks, the miners carried in more than 1,000 cubic feet of tamping to ensure that the force of the explosion would go up rather than down the tunnel. Pleasants's men had surpassed themselves with this Yankee ingenuity.

The entrance to the Union tunnel

took place on June 22–23, as units from two Federal corps moved against the Weldon Railroad but were repulsed when Confederate troops found and exploited a gap in their lines.

Federal soldiers in the 48th Pennsylvania regiment, a unit that included a number of coal miners, convinced their colonel that they could dig a tunnel under the Confederate fortifications, pack it with gunpowder, and blow a hole in the enemy line. General Ambrose E. Burnside, their immediate corps commander, enthusiastically supported the plan, but professional engineers at army headquarters pooh-poohed the idea. Still, the men of the 48th started construction of a tunnel, using ingenuity and brawn to complete the project. Its main shaft was 511 feet in length. Burnside gathered his corps and was promised support from the rest of the army. He planned to use a black division as a spearhead for the assault, but was overruled and told to use his white troops. Burnside had his division commanders draw straws, and as it happened the general with the least experience got the short straw. As a result, even though the explosion of the mine on July 30 was a spectacular success, Burnside's troops bungled the attack. While initially successful, it was contained by Confederate reinforcements, and the Yankees were forced to retreat. This battle, known both as the Crater and the Mine Explosion, cost Grant 5,000 casualties.

In order to divert Federal troops from Petersburg, General Lee sent one of his corps into the Shenandoah Valley to reinforce its outnumbered defenders. Then, after General Jubal Early's troops had driven the Yankees out of the Valley, Early launched a raid across the Potomac River into Maryland. His troops approached the Washington fortifications but were too weak to seize the city, because troops from Grant's army arrived to bolster

Map of corridor between Fredericksburg and Petersburg, Virginia

its defenses. The resulting Shenandoah Valley campaign ended with a complete Confederate defeat in October.

In the meantime, Lee and Grant sparred at Petersburg. Between August 18–21, troops from Warren's Fifth Corps led an advance to the Weldon Railroad. Although his men suffered heavier losses than the Confederate defenders, Warren managed to erect fortifications and held on to his territorial gain, severing the rail line at Globe Tavern.

Another Union expedition took place in late September, when troops from two corps moved west to divert attention from Butler's planned attack on Richmond. Fighting took place from September 30 to October 2, but the Union expeditions only lengthened the lines without making appreciable gains. Another combat occurred on October 27, when Southern defenders repelled Union attacks along the Boydton Plank Road.

After winter brought an end to active operations, Grant's troops struck in February 1865 at Hatcher's Run, but were again deflected from the Southside Railroad. But by now Lee's men were beginning to desert, and he feared that the overwhelming number of Union troops would crush his troops when spring weather dried the roads. So on March 25, General John B. Gordon's men assailed the Union siege lines, capturing Fort Stedman in a desperate bid to break through.

Union reinforcements drove Gordon's men back. Reacting to this victory, Grant sent his cavalry commander, Philip Sheridan, supported by Warren's corps, west to the White Oak Road. On March 31–April 1, Sheridan won a decisive victory, crushing George Pickett's troops at Five Forks and sealing the fate of Petersburg.

Sheridan's victory meant that the railroads were now vulnerable. On April 2, Grant ordered an attack on Petersburg's fortifications. Troops from the Sixth Corps scored a decisive breakthrough, forcing Lee to abandon his lines and retreat. Richmond, now left vulnerable, also was abandoned and occupied by Union troops on April 3. Appomattox was now less than a week away.

Did You Know?

At Petersburg—a strategic railroad hub that provided supplies for the Confederacy's capital city of Richmond—the war saw its longest fought campaign. The Siege of Petersburg was nine-and-a-half-months long and had the largest number of U.S. Colored Troops fighting for their freedom. In all, there were 70,000 casualties. Those who died on the battlefields around Petersburg were temporarily buried where they fell. Union soldiers were later buried at Poplar Grove National Cemetery, while Confederate soldiers were sent to the historic Blandford Cemetery.

PETERSBURG

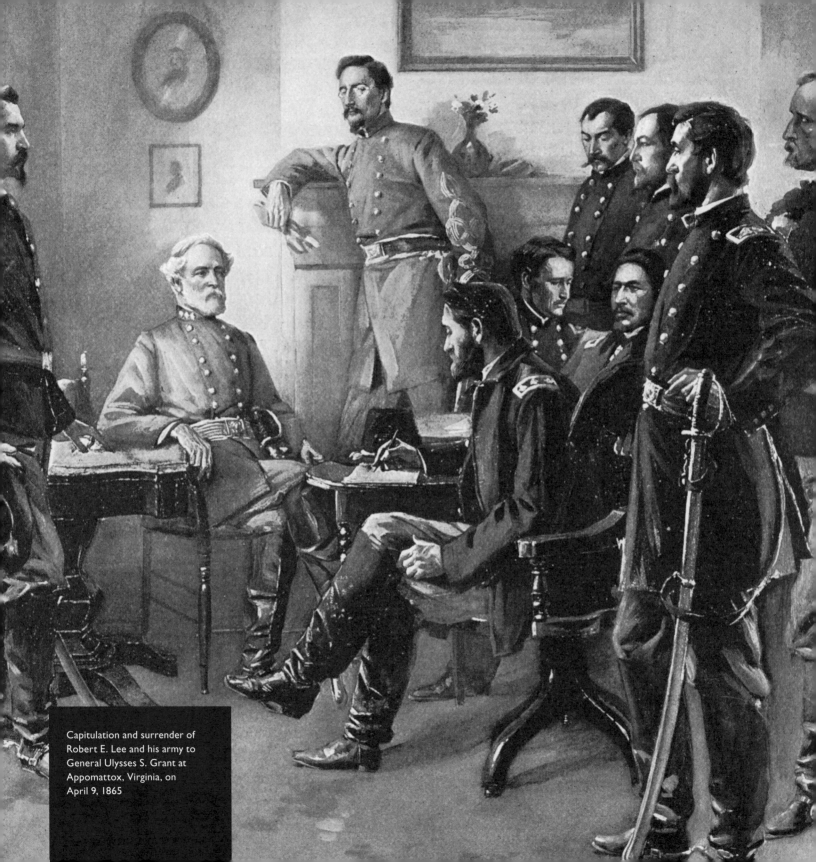

Capitulation and surrender of Robert E. Lee and his army to General Ulysses S. Grant at Appomattox, Virginia, on April 9, 1865

APPOMATTOX

END OF THE WAR

VISITOR INFORMATION

Name Appomattox Court House

Classification National Historical Park

Established June 18, 1930. Transferred from War Department August 10, 1933; redesignated August 13, 1935; April 15, 1954. Boundary changes: February 23, 1939; October 21, 1976; December 3, 1980; October 27, 1992

Contact Highway 24, P.O. Box 218, Appomattox, VA 24522

Phone 434-352-8987, ext. 226

Website www.nps.gov/apco

Acreage 1,774.74 (Federal: 1,679.80; Nonfederal: 94.94)

Points of Focus Appomattox County Jail, Appomattox Court House, Clover Hill Tavern, Mariah Wright House, McLean House, Meeks' Store, Tavern Guest House, Woodson Law Office

Tours/Paths Self-guided walking tours, 6-mile History Trail, McLean House tours

Hours Visitor center open daily from 8:30 a.m. to 5:00 p.m. Closed Thanksgiving Day, December 25, and January 1

Park Fee Memorial Day to Labor Day: $4 per person, maximum $10 per vehicle. Labor Day to Memorial Day: $3 per person, maximum $5 per vehicle, $15 annual pass. Free for ages 16 and under

Programs Two 15-minute audio visual presentations, Living History programs (summer season only)

Facilities Visitor center, museum, bookstore, picnic areas

Union troops breached the Confederate defenses of Petersburg on April 2, 1865. General Lee then decided to abandon Petersburg and Richmond, move west about 40 miles to Amelia Court House to gather supplies, then turn south in an attempt to unite with General Joseph E. Johnston's Southern army in North Carolina. Then, Lee thought, their combined strength could defeat General William T. Sherman's army before Grant's and Sherman's forces united.

But when Lee arrived at Amelia Court House, he found no supplies as anticipated. Worse, Grant kept up a close pursuit in an effort to prevent Lee from moving south. On April 6 General Sheridan's Yankees caught up with the Confederate rear-guard at Saylor's Creek. Union assaults overwhelmed the outnumbered defenders, 7,000 of whom surrendered, effectively destroying Lee's Second Corps.

Lee continued his retreat as his army melted away. Food was scarce and many soldiers, realizing that their cause was doomed, began to desert. But many thousands remained loyal to their great chief and marched

General Ulysses S. Grant

APPOMATTOX COURT HOUSE NATIONAL HISTORICAL PARK ★ APPOMATTOX, VIRGINIA

The reconstructed McLean House

onward even as Union troops, marching along parallel roads to the south, maneuvered into position in front of Lee's men. Lee hesitated to attack, then sent a message to Grant, asking for terms of surrender. Lee realized that his outnumbered army was virtually surrounded, short on supplies and ammunition, and in danger of annihilation.

Currier & Ives lithograph of Lee's surrender

Lee and Grant met in Wilmer McLean's house in the tiny village of Appomattox Court House. After some discussion, Lee agreed to Grant's generous terms. His men would all be paroled as prisoners of war and sent home. Men who owned horses would be allowed to take them along to help with spring planting. Officers would retain their swords, but all firearms, flags, and cannon would be surrendered. The official surrender ceremony took place on April 12, when approximately 28,000 Confederate soldiers laid down their arms and went home. Other Confederate armies followed suit and by mid-May, most Southern troops had given up the struggle and the Civil War was over.

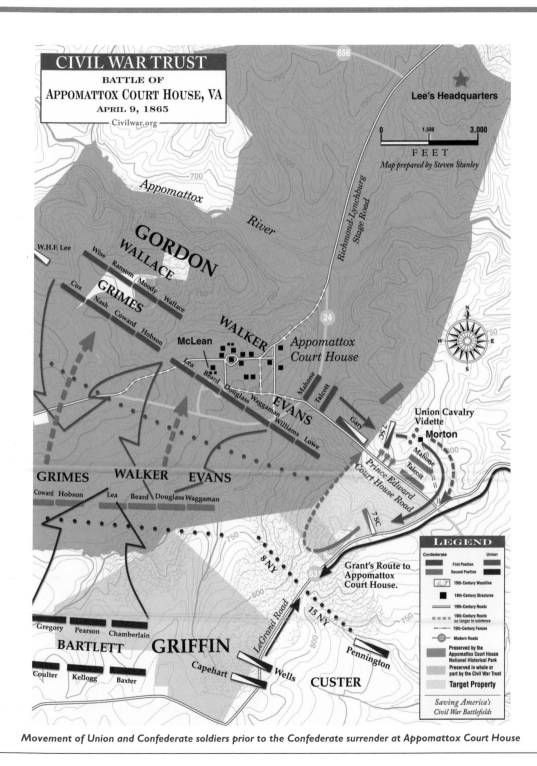

CIVIL WAR TRUST

BATTLE OF
APPOMATTOX COURT HOUSE, VA
APRIL 9, 1865

Civilwar.org

★ Lee's Headquarters

0   1,500   3,000
FEET

Map prepared by Steven Stanley

Appomattox River

Richmond-Lynchburg Stage Road

GORDON
WALLACE

W.H.F. Lee
Wise
Ransom
Moody
Wallace

GRIMES
Cox
Nash
Coward
Hobson

WALKER
McLean
Lea
Beard
Douglass
Waggaman
EVANS
Williams
Lowe
Mahone
Talcott

Appomattox
Court House

24

Gary

Union Cavalry
Vidette
Morton

Mahone
Talcott

7 SC

GRIMES
Coward Hobson
WALKER
Lea Beard
EVANS
Douglass Waggaman

Prince Edward
Court House Road

7 SC

LEGEND

Confederate		Union
	First Position	
	Second Position	

19th-Century Woodline
19th-Century Structures
19th-Century Roads
19th-Century Roads no longer in existence
19th-Century Fences
Modern Roads
Preserved by the Appomattox Court House National Historical Park
Preserved in whole or part by the Civil War Trust
Target Property

8 NY

63

Grant's Route to
Appomattox
Court House.

15 NY

LeGrand Road

Pennington

Gregory Pearson Chamberlain
BARTLETT   **GRIFFIN**
Coulter Kellogg Baxter
Capehart Wells
CUSTER

Saving America's
Civil War Battlefields

Movement of Union and Confederate soldiers prior to the Confederate surrender at Appomattox Court House

Did You Know?

Robert E. Lee's surrender on Sunday, April 10, 1865, at Appomattox Court House, Virginia, was remarkably cordial. Ulysses S. Grant deferred to Lee on the location of the meeting, and the two men spoke for nearly a half hour while Grant, who later admitted to being embarrassed to ask Lee for surrender, waited for Lee to broach the subject. Grant agreed to allow the Confederates to keep their horses and immediately sent 25,000 rations to the starving Southern troops. Both Lee and Grant acted with such grace during the meeting that it was dubbed "The Gentlemen's Agreement."

APPOMATTOX

This Kurz & Allison print depicts the capitulation and surrender of General Robert E. Lee and his army to Lieutenant General Ulysses S. Grant on April 9, 1865, at Appomattox Court House, Virginia.

CREDITS

COVER

Top image: Library of Congress Prints and Photographs Division

Bottom image: C. Kurt Holter/Shutterstock.com

INTERIOR

AP/Wide World Photo/Lisa Billings: 149b

AP/Wide World Photo/The Leaf-Chronicle, Greg Williamson: 47a

Civil War Trust: 44 (http://www.civilwar.org/battlefields/wilsonscreek/maps/wilsonscreekmap.html), 59a (http://www.civilwar.org/battlefields/shiloh/maps/shilohmap.html), 85 (http://www.civilwar.org/battlefields/antietam/maps/antietammap1.html), 135b (http://www.civilwar.org/battlefields/chickamauga/chickamauga-maps/), 141(http://www.civilwar.org/battlefields/kennesawmountain/kennesaw-maps/kennesawmap.html), 155(http://www.civilwar.org/battlefields/appomattox-courthouse/maps/appomattoxmap.html)

C. Theodore Lyon Collection: 148a

Courtesy National Park Service, Museum Management Program and Ford Theater National Historical Park. US Treasury Guards Flag, FOTH 22. www.cr.nps.gov/museum/exhibits/flags/foth22.htm: 23

Courtesy National Park Service, Museum Management Program and Fort Sumter Historical Park. Palmetto Flag, FOSU 1861. www.cr.nps.gov/museum/exhibits/flags/fosu1861.htm: 26a

Courtesy National Park Service, Museum Management Program and Fort Sumter National Historical Park. Storm Flag, FOSU9. www.cr.nps.gov/museum/exhibits/flags/fosu9.htm: 12

Courtesy Independence National Historical Park: 26b

Courtesy of Mark H. Dunkelman: 121b

Courtesy of Richard A. Sauers: 91c, 104b

Getty Images: 5a, 13, 16, 19, 54, 55, 88, 96b, 108, 111a, 111b, 117, 137, 149a

Library of Congress: 2 (LC-DIG-pga-02051), 3 (LC-DIG-ppmsca-31220), 5 (LC-DIG-ppmsca-32751), 6-7 (08899u), 8a (LC-DIG-cwpb-04048), 8b (LC-DIG-ppmsca-20557), 9b (LC-USZC4-5610), 10 (LC-DIG-pga-03861), 14-15 (LC-USZC4-12419), 18a (cph 3a12898), 18c (LC-USZ62-89569), 22 (LC-USZC4-1761), 24-25 (LC-DIG-pga-01777), 27 (LC-USZC4-528), 29a (LC-USZC2-2663), 30a (LC-DIG-cwpb-03156), 30b (LC-USZC2-2353), 31 (Sumter_vhs00058), 32a (LC-DIG-ppmsca-31705), 32b (LC-DIG-ppmsca-31729), 32c (LC-DIG-ppmsca-31709), 32d (LC-DIG-ppmsca-31813), 32e (LC-DIG-ppmsca-31972) 32f (LC-DIG-ppmsca-31816), 33a (LC-DIG-ppmsca-31959), 33b (LC-DIG-ppmsca-31703), 33c (LC-DIG-ppmsca-31970), 33d (LC-DIG-ppmsca-31715), 33e (LC-DIG-ppmsca-31971), 33f (LC-DIG-ppmsca-31983), 34 (LC-USZC4-1796), 36b (gvhs01_vhs00060), 40-41 (LC-DIG-cwpb-04017), 43 (LC-USZC4-1767), 46 (LC-USZC4-1764), 48

(Donelson2_cw0409100), 49 (Donelson_vhs00078), 51 (LC-USZC4-1330), 52 (LC-DIG-pga-00612), 53b (PeaRidge_cw0116000), 56a (LC-USZC4-1910), 57 (0195-0088-0266), 60-61 (LC-DIG-pga-00540), 62 (LC-DIG-cwpb-00787), 63 (LC-B811-191A), 64 (LC-USZC2-1989), 65 (FortPulaski_vhs00084), 66a (AC0060-0001180), 66b (AC0060-0001174), 66c (AC0060-0001177), 66d (AC0060-0001169), 66e (AC0060-0001175a), 66f (AC0060-0001246a), 66g (AC0060-0001175b), 66h (AC0060-0001246b), 67a (AC0060-0001308), 67b (AC0060-0001309), 67c (LC-DIG-ppmsca-31316), 67d (LC-DIG-ppmsca-32676), 67e (LC-DIG-ppmsca-32634), 68 (LC-B8171-471 DLC), 71 (LC-USZ62-110263), 73a (LC-USZC4-1519), 73b, 74-75 (Richmond_vhs00290), 80a (LC-USZ62-100817), 80b (LC-USZ62-93979), 82b (LC-USZ62-11682), 83 (LC-DIG-ppmsca-11364), 86-87 (LC-DIG-pga-01841), 90a (LC-USZC4-1757), 91a (LC-USZC4-1976), 92a (LC-DIG-cwpbh-03386), 92b (Fredericksburg_vhs00124), 94b (LC-DIG-pga-01844), 96a (LC-DIG-pga-02746), 97 (Chancellorsville_vhs00226), 98-99 (LC-DIG-ppmsca-22752),100 (LC-DIG-cwph-2108), 101 (LC-B811-2582), 102a (LC-USZC2-2510), 103a (LC-DIG-pga-02189), 104a (LC-USZC4-1768), 106a (LC-USZ62-50846), 106b (LC-DIG-cwpbh-03133), 106c (LC-USZ62-124355), 106d (LC-DIG-cwpbh-03118), 107a (LC-DIG-cwpbh-03218), 107b (LC-DIG-cwpbh-03127), 107c (LC-BH831-1152), 107d (LC-DIG-cwpbh-03239), 109 (LC-DIG-pga-03430), 112 (Vicksburg_cw0283300), 114-115 (LC-USZC4-1754), 118-119 (LC-USZC4-2815), 124 (LC-USZ62-40269), 125a (LC-USZ62-106651), 126 (LC-USZC4-1859), 127 (Gettysburg_cw0330000), 128-129 (LC-DIG-pga-03266), 130 (LC-USZC4-1762), 131 (LC-USZC4-7984), 132a (LC-DIG-cwpb-3432), 135a (LC-DIG-stereo-1s02804), 139 (LC-USZC4-1766), 140 (LC-USZ62-40149), 142 (LC-DIG-cwpb-4232DLC), 143 (HABS, MD, 11-FRED. V, 12-), 144a (LC-USZC4-1766), 144b (LC-DIG-ppmsca-21238), 145 (Monocacy_vhs00170), 146 (LC-USZ62-72083), 148b (LC-DIG-cwpb-4346DLC), 150 (Petersburg_vhs00038), 154b (LC-USZC2-3054), 156-157 (LC-DIG-pga-01895)

National Archives: 37 (165-SB-11), 84b (165-SB-19), 90b (111-B-514)

National Park Service: 20 (FTSU0336), 53a (PERI3142), 70a (RICH0381), 79 (ANTI0924), 89a (FRED6074), 118 (GETT1694), 120 (GETT3421), 154a (APCO0569)

Naval Historical Center: 21 (NH999), 110 (NH 61568)

©New York Public Library: 76-77

Picture Collection, The Branch Libraries, The New York Public Library, Astor, Lenox and Tilden Foundations: 28, 45, 58, 72, 122, 134, 152

Private Collection: 17, 29b, 35, 36a, 37, 38, 47b, 50, 56b, 59, 69, 70b, 78, 84a, 89b, 90b, 91b, 93, 95, 102b, 103b, 116, 121a, 123a, 125b, 133, 136, 138, 139b, 144, 147, 153

Rhode Island State Library, The: 123b

Shay, Art/Time Life Pictures/Getty Images: 18c

Smithsonian Institution: 94

Wisconsin Historical Society: 132b (WHi-4502)